LOOKING BACK
MOVING FORWARD

My Life in the American Labor Movement

JOHN J. SWEENEY

ISBN: 978-1-48359-235-0

For Kennedy, in the hopes that you will continue my fight for a more just world. May you never forget the power of your name.

CONTENTS

FOREWORD

In 1982, not long after I became president of the United Mine Workers of America, the American Federation of State, County and Municipal Employees held a reception for me. A man approached, shook my hand and started to ask me questions. I liked him immediately. You couldn't mistake his humility and genuine interest. He congratulated me on my recent election so sincerely and with such joy that you'd think he had won, too. Maybe we both had, because that day began a truly remarkable and rewarding friendship. The man was John J. Sweeney, then president of the Service Employees International Union and, always, one of the few people who truly lives that old adage... "it's better to give than to receive."

Years later, when I was secretary-treasurer of the AFL-CIO and John was president, we were running to catch a plane. A young mother in front of us with a baby and stroller dropped an armload of her things. John didn't simply stop to help her. He put down everything he carried. He helped her gather her belongings. He focused all his energy on making sure she would have an easier time traveling with her child. And we missed our plane, which was fine. We caught the next flight. But that was John in a nutshell. He embodied his values every day, and in every way. I have always found that impressive.

Over his life as a labor leader, some folks will recall John as the man with the bullhorn who shut down Washington bridges at rush hour to get his way with employers. In New York, he led strikes that virtually paralyzed the city. He made history as the upstart who overturned the leadership of the AFL-CIO in an unprecedented coup, and I can tell you he was the right man at the right time. All that is true, but an incomplete picture of the complex and gentle soul I know and admire. He chose a life in the labor movement as an expression of deeply held moral convictions about social justice. Most of the adversaries he faced in his career probably knew John as a soft-spoken, serious advocate for working people. In his low-key style, armed with facts and figures, he worked hard to win the best deal possible for the workers he represented. But if an employer balked or refused to bargain in good faith, John was ready and willing to "take it to the streets."

This memoir reveals a side of John that most people have not seen: the spiritual life that brought him into the labor movement as a young man and motivated his career. In the union household where he grew up in New York, raised by his Irish immigrant parents, the values of family, faith and union were central. He entered a seminary after college with the thought of going into a religious life. But he found his calling through the priests he met at the Xavier Institute of Industrial Relations in Manhattan, men of faith who taught classes for union leaders and who actively supported workers in the struggle for justice. John knew then that he wanted to work in the union movement. His decision was driven by his belief that union organizing was one of the best ways to fulfill the values in which he had been raised. His career in the labor movement was a spiritual calling.

After our first meeting in 1982, John set an example for all of us in steadily building SEIU into the largest union in the AFL-CIO. His style was not flashy, but he got results. He built a lot of powerful relationships across the labor movement. He earned respect. By the early 1990s, John and I were among a group of dissident union presidents who saw that the AFL-CIO had become moribund. When we felt our concerns were not being taken seriously by the AFL-CIO's leaders, John became the clear choice to lead the dissenters. We challenged the incumbent leadership and went on to win election at the 1995 AFL-CIO convention. I am honored to have served as secretary-treasurer under his leadership. We worked closely during his 14 years as president.

I would say that John's success as a national labor leader was grounded in his enormous respect for individual working people. He listens, asks questions and then takes action. Even when he was back in New York City, building the janitors' union into the largest local in the SEIU, he got his greatest satisfactions from conversations with workers about jobs, family, and hopes for the future. His respect for others is not constrained by a person's race, sex, religion, national origin, or sexual orientation. He helped institutionalize that respect by expanding and diversifying union leadership ranks, first at SEIU and then as president of the AFL-CIO. In contrast to many old-line union officials, he encouraged his diverse staff members to bring new ideas to the table for discussion, and he was always ready to try innovative ways to engage the grassroots membership so vital to the health of our movement. At the AFL-CIO today, we continue to build on many of the organizing and political strategies that John initiated during his years as president.

When we look back on the lives and careers of great women and men, it can be easy to overlook the fact that there was a regular person in the middle of it all. John guided the American labor movement through a tough time for working people. Despite the pressures on him, he consistently hewed closely to his values. He treated everyone decently, and wasn't always treated with the same decency in return. Nevertheless, his faith remained unchanged. Even in contentious exchanges, John listened. I have found, through my friendship with John, that listening is not enough. The response is important, too. The response can bring people together, or push people apart. John always brought people together. That spirit is immensely valuable in America today. John Sweeney is my close friend and brother, and like so many others I am better off because of him.

Richard L. Trumka

Trumka is president of the AFL-CIO.

1

COMMUNITY OF IMMIGRANTS: WHERE MY LIFE'S WORK BEGAN

Growing up, the three most important things were our family, the church, and my father's union. Like so many other Irish immigrant families, we knew that without our family, there would be no love; without our church, there would be no redemption; and without my father's union, there would be no food on the table.

A Working-Class Neighborhood. When I was young, my family lived in a community called Tremont in St. Joseph's parish in the Bronx. Our neighbors came from many different backgrounds: a mix of Irish, German, Italian, and Jewish families. Our Bronx community was filled with hard-working people who firmly believed they could make life better for themselves and their families – people like my parents, James Sweeney and Agnes McMorrow Sweeney, who emigrated from Ireland in 1929, so full of their Irish-Catholic faith that they brought my brother, my sisters, and me into the world despite the Great Depression. Our home was on the second floor of a walk-up tenement. We did not have a telephone; my parents made calls on the public phone at the candy store. We had no car; either, we walked or took the subway or bus.

I do not believe it is a coincidence that three of the AFL-CIO's five presidents have hailed from the Bronx. I am proud to be part of that group of New Yorkers who came to lead the world's greatest labor federation. The Bronx had been New York City's fastest growing borough in the 1920s, with thousands of small factories and an army of skilled workers – carpenters, house painters, garment workers, machinists, brick masons – who kept the neighborhoods humming. But when the Great Depression hit in 1929, the year my parents arrived, things came to a standstill: Construction was down and evictions were up. Although work opportunities were slim, my parents found a solid community built around the church and the neighborhood, and by the time I was born in 1934, they were managing fairly well.

As a child of the New Deal era, I saw at an early age that our government had the power to make our lives better. For many Bronx families, Franklin Delano Roosevelt was seen as a savior when he was elected president in 1932. His New Deal projects, like the Works Progress Administration, put people to work repairing roads and bridges and constructing public parks and buildings. We were also fortunate to have effective local Democratic Party leaders like Edward J. Flynn, an early Roosevelt supporter, who made sure that the Bronx got its share of those public works programs. As a kid, I managed to see President Roosevelt in person as his open-air limousine drove up Tremont Avenue during his last campaign for president. I was with my Dad. The president was waving to the people, and as I looked around I saw adults with tears running down their faces. It made such a strong impression on me.

A Family of Humble Origins and Rich Values. I came from a modest background, but in my home, we never lacked for tradition and values. Growing up, my two sisters, my brother, and I enjoyed very happy days.

My parents were kind and compassionate people who made sure we did not want for anything. They were natives of the small western Irish County of Leitrim and they never forgot their origins. The towns they grew up in, Ballinamore and Drumkeerin, did not offer much opportunity, but they were rich in Irish culture, especially Irish music. Both of my parents had good memories of Ireland and passed on their love of all things Irish to us.

In fact thanks to my mother I can lay claim to some real Irish rebel blood. Through her and the McMorrow clan, I am related to the Irish patriot Sean McDermott. He was one of the leaders of the 1916 Easter Rebellion, which sought to liberate Ireland from British rule, and he signed the famous Easter Week Proclamation. He was executed by a British firing squad for his part in the rebellion.

Our home was filled with music and a sense of happiness and hope for the future despite the tough times of the Depression. I grew up listening to Irish programs on the radio. On Sunday nights especially, our whole family listened to news from Ireland, the goings on in our New York community, and of course all those Irish songs by performers such as the McNulty Family, who came from my parents' neck of the woods in the old country. I read the Irish newspapers that came into the house, and in grammar school and high school I marched in the St. Patrick's Day parade. I enjoyed listening to my aunts and uncles chat with my parents about Ireland. The long history of the Irish helped me and my family to think of the Great Depression as simply a temporary chapter in a young nation's history.

Irish History, Heritage, and Faith. When you study labor history, the Irish are on almost every page. Their hands helped build America. Irish immigrants dug coal that powered the Industrial Revolution, and they helped construct the canals, railroads, and bridges that revolutionized transportation in the mid-19th century. Like every new immigrant group, they did the hardest, dirtiest work that usually commanded the lowest wage. Maybe that is why they understood from the start that nobody does it alone.

The Irish believe in being there for each other, especially in times of need. That is why we built institutions that help us help each other – and not just for ourselves alone. We built churches with active parishes and a strong community, where people are welcomed into the world when they are born and given a proper burial when they die. Our people created innumerable civic and charitable organizations that serve our broader communities, not just those with Irish roots. And of course, Irish hands have done much to make and shape the American labor movement.

The belief that built our unions – the inherent dignity of every person and his or her work – is in the best tradition of the Irish history, heritage, and faith that surrounded me as I was growing up.

Insights from My Catholic Education. Thanks to years of Catholic education, first at St. Joseph's in the Bronx, St. Barnabas in Yonkers, and then Cardinal Hayes High School, an all-boys school in the Bronx, I had a good background in Catholic social teaching. I learned about Rerum Novarum, Pope Leo XIII's 1891 encyclical that addressed the conditions of workers in an industrializing world. It was written at a time of violent industrial unrest, and the pope made it clear that there could be no peace without justice. He also taught that there was dignity in labor, that a "just" wage should be enough to support a family, and that workers and employers ought to be free to negotiate and agree upon fair conditions. Those ideas made a lot of sense to me. I also became familiar with the 1931 encyclical, Quadragesimo Anno, by Pope Pius XI, that built upon Pope Leo's work and linked the idea of social justice to the need to pursue the common good.

Meeting with Pope John Paul II in 2000. The Pope taught that worker solidarity is a key dimension of the human condition, and as a native of Poland, he was particularly supportive of the AFL-CIO's work to foster free trade unionism there.

These teachings should not seem radical. But unfortunately – even today, here in our own country – the basic rights of working people are never secure. These rights and values must still be fought for, as they were in the late 19th century when leaders like Samuel Gompers of the American Federation of Labor and Terence Powderly of the Knights of Labor first sought to educate and organize America's working people.

A Union Family. Someone once asked me who I admired most in life, and it did not take me long to answer, "My father." He is the one who gave me the roots of my trade union interests. James Sweeney drove a bus in the Bronx. He was a member of Local 100 of the Transport Workers Union, or TWU, whose president was the legendary labor leader Mike Quill. One of my father's runs was in the north Bronx, the No. 4 bus, which would take him about two blocks from our home. My mother would send me to meet him with the lunch she had made him. He would park the bus, and while he had his break and ate his lunch, I sat on a passenger seat and we talked: about the bus or his work or whatever was on his mind. When he got up to stretch his legs, I would jump into the driver's seat. Sitting behind the wheel (with no key in the ignition, of course), I felt like the king of the mountain. Those are dear memories.

During our summer holidays, my mother would take the four of us kids on day trips to Orchard Beach, a great public park in the Bronx. The biggest treat of all was when Dad came out and met us at the end of his working day. We would be waiting for him at the end of his route. Dad would take off his uniform jacket and hat and join us for an ice cream, a soda pop, or maybe a hot dog. I have not forgotten those good times and our good fortune as a working-class family.

I was also learning that the labor movement had done much to make our sense of security and happiness possible. To this day I do not take for granted the benefits my family enjoyed thanks to the early struggles and sacrifices of the men and women who built the labor movement. The struggle for economic justice did not come easy then, and protecting those gains does not come easy today. But it is vital to protect them so working people and their families can continue to enjoy the benefits of the American Dream as my own family did.

The Union Difference. I was not very old when I discovered the difference it made to be in a union. My mother was a domestic worker and had to depend on her employers' good will as far as wages and benefits were concerned. Some of her employers were decent, and some were not. Before I was born, she had worked for the Lewisohns, a very wealthy, very generous family who lived in Manhattan. When Mrs. Lewisohn vacationed in Europe during the summer, she took my mother with her as her maid, and she gave my mother a week or two of vacation to go visit her mother in Ireland. But when my mother went back to work cleaning houses after my youngest brother started school, she was not always so lucky. There were no benefits of any kind, and if she got paid with a bad check, there was no place to turn for help. She had to work it out herself or she did not get paid.

My father, on the other hand, could count on his union contract, union benefits, and fairly regular wage increases. In fact by 1945, just 16 years after their arrival in this country, he and my mother were able to save up a little money and buy a house in Yonkers, just outside of the Bronx. It was a very modest two-family house that had been foreclosed on during the Depression. The house was old and it needed work, but to own our own home in a nice residential neighborhood was quite an achievement at the time – one that a union job helped make possible.

My father's union contract provided health care benefits and paid vacations. I knew that when the contract expired, he might get an additional day of vacation under the new contract – a day he might use to take us over to Rockaway Beach in Queens. My father would then lean back in his chair and say, "Thank God for Mike Quill and the Transport Workers Union."

Mike Quill in Action. Even as a kid I was fascinated by the outspoken leader of my father's union. I was lucky enough to see him in action when my father let me accompany him to the contract negotiation meetings. There could be a thousand people milling around and Mike Quill, an Irish immigrant, would be up there with his big voice and strong Irish brogue. People used to say that his brogue got stronger the closer he came to a strike.

Mike Quill was a visionary in my humble opinion, as he was one of the first union leaders to realize how TV could be used to gain free publicity. I remember one meeting in the early 1950s where he had a TV camera recording the proceedings and a big empty chair, very ornate, like a chair for royalty. He said, "You're wondering who that chair is for? Well, I invited the mayor." Vincent Impellitteri was the mayor's name. "I invited Impy, the mayor, to be here today to give us a report on the negotiations. But I don't think he's got the guts to come into this hall because he's afraid of all of you folks. He's afraid, and rightly so, that you might throw him out. But I just want him to see the chair, the nice chair that I provided for him."

Attending these union meetings as a kid, I learned how the union can be more than a mechanism for raising wages and resolving grievances; it can be a creative social movement. I came to understand how being part of an effective labor organization was so important in protecting workers' rights. And I learned that political action also played a vital role. What working people win at the bargaining table, we can lose in the political process.

Political Awakening. From my earliest days I had a strong interest in politics. And like everything else, it started at home. Whether I was reading the political column in my father's union newspaper, or following local elections, I learned from a young age how important it was to elect people who supported working-class issues, such as increasing the minimum wage. President Roosevelt was a prime example. FDR's use of public funds to get us out of the Depression offered hope to so many ordinary people who were struggling. Interestingly, much of Roosevelt's New Deal had its roots in his years as governor of New York State, before I was born. When Wall Street crashed in 1929, his first year as governor, he created a statewide relief program that would be a model for his later New Deal emergency relief measures. Roosevelt's state secretary of labor, Frances Perkins, helped the governor establish a record of protecting workers' right and would later follow him to Washington as Secretary of Labor.

Although my parents went to political meetings, they did not have the time or the education to go out and work on a campaign. But thanks to them, I had that early interest and desire: I knew that it was important to support the person you thought was going to do the best for working people. And by the time I was in high school, I was taking every chance that came my way to get involved.

My father would get postcards from the union's COPE committee – the Committee on Political Education – asking him to go campaign for somebody. With his permission I spent a Saturday with TWU bus drivers handing out leaflets or tooling around the Bronx in a sound truck. When one of the drivers asked if I wanted to take the microphone, I said, "Sure. What do I say?" The driver said, "Just look at what you're handing out there." And so I took the mike and blared, "You know next Tuesday is Election Day. I hope that you're all going to vote for Bill O'Dwyer for mayor. He's the best man for working people." It was the first time I spoke into a microphone, and I liked it.

That was the beginning of my being active in politics. I started on the streets handing out literature for Democratic candidates for local office that we could count on to support union positions. This campaigning helped me later in working with people, speaking in public, and understanding the importance of paying attention to details. But most of all it taught me how to listen to people and their concerns.

First Taste of Union Organizing. I got my first chance at union leadership when I helped organize the caddies at Dunwoodie Golf Course, in Yonkers, where I worked as a teenager. We caddies were demanding a pay increase of 75 cents for every bag we carried. To prove we were serious, we stopped work at the bottom of a hill on the golf course. After a while the golfers understood we were on strike, and they sent a committee to negotiate with us. We got our full 75-cents-per-bag increase.

In those days I had all kinds of jobs, from stocking shelves at Safeway (under a union contract); to floor walking at S.H. Kress, a 5 & 10 cent store; to filling in graves at the Gate of Heaven Cemetery (another union job). I would do whatever I could to have a buck in my pocket, as they say.

In this picture I am standing (at left) with two of my co-workers at one of my earliest union jobs, filling in graves at Gate of Heaven Cemetery in Hawthorne, N.Y.

At the same time I was learning a lot about the problems that workers so often faced and how tough it was for them when they first got organized or when they were forced to strike. At the cemetery, we would all have lunch, and I would listen to these guys talk about their work issues. I would listen to what they said when the union contract was coming close to expiration and what they wanted in the next contract. I had my own ideas, of course, but then I was more interested in learning about how they felt. Would they go out on strike if they had to? Invariably, I heard, "I can't afford to go out on strike." I would say, "Well, then, you've got to push for a settlement, but it's got to be a decent settlement." I encouraged them to talk with others who felt the same way they did, and definitely to go to the next membership meeting. Then they would tell me what went on at the meeting. These discussions were eye-openers for me.

Continuing My Social Justice Education. When I entered Iona College in 1951, I majored in economics, which seemed like a practical choice, but I kept up my strong interest in Catholic moral and social teaching. Iona was a relatively new college, established in nearby New Rochelle by the Christian Brothers in 1940. The Christian Brothers believed in the power of education to change the world, and through Iona they hoped to give working-class students like me the opportunity to expand our horizons while we improved our chances of making a good living. They did a good job. What I had learned through experience about the labor movement's value to working people like my father, I now learned at an intellectual level through my classes at Iona College.

I also like to credit the Christian Brothers at Iona for teaching me it is better to ask for forgiveness than to ask for permission, a good lesson for a future labor leader! When I received my diploma – the first in my immediate family – I was confident that if I worked hard, played by the rules, and stood up for what is right, I would succeed in life and be able to give something back, as my father and the Christian Brothers had taught me.

I was not ready to take on the world just yet, though. My interest in the church and my faith were so strong that I followed up college with a few years in the seminary, first in Toronto and then in Pennsylvania. I was searching to discover what I really wanted to do with my life. In addition to my interest in the labor movement, I had a strong interest in the work the church was doing in hospitals and schools, as well as its missionary work. It seemed to me that in a vocation or calling related to a religious life, I could do very much the same thing whether I had a job as a priest or a job as a union organizer. To explore that path, more education would be necessary. So for two years I studied Latin, Greek, philosophy, and theology.

Then I came to a decision: I had pursued my religious vocation as much as I wanted to, and I was going to follow up on my opportunities in the labor movement. I was not sorry for the seminary experience but had come to the conclusion that I would eventually like to be married and have a family. I knew that my strong religious training and strong religious spirit would stay with me.

Work Without a Higher Purpose. Not long after returning from the seminary, I took a job at IBM, working in the market research department. We were focused on a potential market study for the production of small mainframe computers for small public utilities. I had taken a course in statistics at Iona, and I enjoyed this work, especially the computer experience. I also valued working at a major firm, a nonunion firm, and having the opportunity, since I was in research, to mingle with workers who had a lot of experience. That gave me an opportunity to talk with them about what they thought of labor unions. While I found the work at IBM to be intellectually stimulating, I found something to be missing. I knew this work would not be my career, and I think many others realized that, too.

Connecting Family, Faith, and Unions. While I realized after graduating from college that I was not quite cut out for the priesthood, I still felt compelled to continue my spiritual and religious education and pursue my interest in social justice. I began studying Catholic social teaching with Father Philip Carey, a Jesuit who ran the Xavier Institute of Industrial Relations in Manhattan. These classes help to give me a sense of purpose and community that I lacked working at a big corporation. The Xavier program was geared towards full-time workers who wanted to be active in their unions. It was a night school that taught the nuts and bolts of the labor movement with classes on labor history, parliamentary procedure, and labor law. This was a very practical education. We learned how to speak in public, how to write resolutions, how to bargain collectively and hold our own, whether the subject was economic policy, industrial relations, or ethics.

But it was a spiritual education, too. The priests at Xavier saw Christ in the workers; they viewed the work of laboring in the mines, or building houses, or operating elevators as a vocation. Father Carey and his assistant Father John Corridan – who, incidentally, was the model for the priest played by Karl Malden in *On the Waterfront* – would tell us that we work out our salvation in this world. We do not save souls on our knees, we save souls by prayer and work with others. Father Carey and Father Corridan thought nothing of walking a picket line with strikers, and the work they did with the Longshoremen's union was really historic. As long as their health held up, they remained at the grassroots struggle.

From them, I learned more about how family, faith, and union are connected in Catholic social teaching – a more in depth version of the values I had been taught at home. I came to understand that work is another form of worship. Through work, we share in God's creation that is the foundation and ordering of life.

I also learned that working people have God-given rights, and that there is a moral connection that links the church, the rights of workers, and economic justice. And I learned more about the Catholic Church's active role in the early days of the trade union movement. Wherever there was an organizing campaign or a strike, from the struggles in the mines of Colorado to the sit-down strikes in Detroit, fighting labor priests took their place beside workers on the frontlines of the battle for social justice.

Most of all, Father Carey taught me that a union must be a movement and a mission, not a business or a bureaucracy. He and the others in the program made me realize that organizing new union members is not only an institutional necessity but an ethical imperative. It is a practical example of the fortunate using their strength and their assets to help their less fortunate brothers and sisters.

Now I was really determined to find a union job where I could put these principles into practice.

2

FINDING MY CALLING: MY START
IN THE LABOR MOVEMENT

With Father Carey's help, after only about a year at IBM, I got a job in the research department of the International Ladies' Garment Workers' Union – a forerunner of UNITE HERE – and was able to become a "union guy" again. Even though I would be taking a cut in salary, I could not get there fast enough.

When I went to work at the ILGWU in 1956, I became part of a union that had been doing groundbreaking organizing of garment industry workers since its founding in 1900. One of this country's most horrific workplace tragedies – the 1911 Triangle Shirtwaist Factory fire – killed 146 young immigrant women who were trapped inside a New York City factory that the union was trying to organize. Their escape was blocked because the company had locked its sweat shop doors to keep employees from mingling in the stairwells. That fire spurred the ILGWU's growth and led to the formation of progressive coalitions between the ILGWU, social reformers, and politicians such as Al Smith, the New York State legislator and later governor.

Those coalitions would help shape progressive public policies on labor issues for years to come. The coalitions born of that tragic fire led to new safety and workers' compensation laws in New York State, and they would later influence national labor policies when New York's governor, Franklin D. Roosevelt, became president of the United States in 1932. President Roosevelt's secretary of labor, Frances Perkins, had been a young pro-labor activist in New York at the time of the Triangle fire and would later say that "the Triangle Shirtwaist Factory Fire was the day the New Deal began."

I, of course, admired the ILGWU's pioneering achievements in improving wages, hours, and working conditions in the garment industry, and so I was proud to start what became my career in the labor movement when I began my work in their research department.

David Dubinsky's ILGWU. David Dubinsky was president of the ILGWU when I joined the staff. He was a powerhouse both within the union and nationally. President since 1932, he had helped maintain the ILGWU following a serious internal fight with a communist faction in the 1920s, and in the 1930s he took advantage of New Deal opportunities to grow the union's membership. Dubinsky was also a political giant: He helped organize the American Labor Party to support President Roosevelt; the Liberal Party (when he thought the communists had too much influence in the ALP); and, in 1947, Americans for Democratic Action, an independent political organization. He was a great example of a socially conscious, politically active, militant labor leader.

The research department was an important entity at the ILGWU, and Lazare Teper, the research director, was a formidable boss. A Russian immigrant, he was a well-respected labor economist who had founded the research department in 1937. By the time I knew him, he was very active in the minimum-wage discussions in the United States, as well as in Central America and the Caribbean. He was often called to testify for a wage increase when union contracts were being negotiated. He was brilliant, and I admired him greatly.

There were about five of us in the research department who kept up to date on current economic trends. The goal was to have material available to prepare local unions for any situation that came up in bargaining sessions. We kept a collection of the major bargaining agreements and when an affiliate took on a new issue or a new benefit, we would make that information available to others who wanted to negotiate something similar.

The Power of Facts and Figures. This research work was a real education for me. The experience I got working on collective bargaining and on social legislation issues gave me a solid background for all my future work. And it gave me an opportunity to give back to Father Carey and the Xavier Labor School, because I gained enough knowledge and experience to return to the classroom as an instructor.

In my brief time with the Garment Workers, I came to appreciate the importance of thorough research and communications in advancing the interests of our members. And I can point to Lazare Teper for that. Solid facts and figures plus the opportunity to communicate our position to the public – those were as important as being well organized on the picket lines. Research also enabled us to build the support of those in elected office and their staffs, who could be powerful advocates for us and who could line up votes on the legislation that we needed.

Working at the ILGWU also broadened my political education. The union had a strong political program and held major rallies for the Democratic presidential nominee in the garment district in Manhattan. Tens of thousands of workers would show up, not just from the Ladies' Garment Workers but from other union workplaces, and also the public at large. I went to those rallies for a number of years – David Dubinsky encouraged me to go.

Standing Up to Power. My job was not always smooth sailing, though, particularly once I joined the ILGWU staff negotiating committee. A number of people had recommended me for that committee, and I wanted to do a good job. So when negotiations started on the staff's union contract, I spoke out on some issues that the staff felt our employer should be more mindful of, such as wages and job titles. The word got back to David Dubinsky that this guy Sweeney was pretty outspoken on things that should be in the contract. One morning I got on the elevator with President Dubinsky. He turned to me – I did not even know that he would recognize me – and asked if I was on the negotiating committee. I said, "Oh yes, I'm really happy to be on the negotiating committee." I was shocked when he replied that I wasn't going to stay happy for long. I thought "Oh, my God. President of the union and he sounds like he's anti-worker." It was an eye-opening experience.

When I told Lazare Teper about what had happened he laughed and told me not to worry about it. "Well," I said, "if I'm going to be on the negotiating committee, I'm going to try to make a contribution. I've got to speak as I hear people speak, including their gripes, whatever they are."

I am glad to say I did not lose my job. And I stayed there until I really did decide to move on. My experience with the ILGWU served me well, and I learned fairly early on in my career that it was good to stand one's ground when the situation merited it, even when dealing with such a powerful figure as David Dubinsky. As the saying goes, "to thine own self be true."

My Run for Democratic District Leader. By 1959 I had been involved with the Democratic Party for a while, and I decided to run for district leader of the Westchester County Democratic Committee. I got my sisters involved in the campaign, ringing doorbells, and they brought some friends, including a friend from the neighborhood, Maureen Power. She had gone to school with my sisters, so we had a lot in common, including an interest in the labor movement. Maureen was working in advertising but she would go on to become a teacher and a member of the United Federation of Teachers. It was not long before we started dating, and the rest is history. We were married in 1962. I always say that was my most successful campaign.

Maureen and I pose for a picture with my parents, John and Agnes Sweeney, at our wedding reception at the Waterwheel in New York.

During my election campaign for district leader – which I won – I learned about the workings of grassroots politics as well as how to engage with people and gain their support. Serving in that party position taught me how the best local political leaders become a direct link for many people to the democratic process. I saw how hard these local leaders worked to advance the cause of ordinary people. I saw how the best of them were able to stay connected to the party's rank and file while maintaining good relationships with our elected officials in the city council and the state legislature. These were lasting lessons for me.

Serving my very diverse community in Yonkers – then made up mostly of Irish, Italians, and Jews, but with more Blacks and Hispanics arriving over time – I learned to get along with so many different men and women, to appreciate the diversity of their ideas. That helped me greatly when I joined the labor movement. The grassroots organizing tools I developed were especially useful in organizing effective lobbying campaigns for workers' legislation. I learned, too, that people want to be respected. They want their concerns to be understood. And if you are their representative, entrusted to work on their behalf, they expect your best efforts in fighting for their interests. When you work hard and earn their trust, you will be all the more effective as an advocate and negotiator because you have their backing.

JFK's Presidential Campaign. It was thanks to a friend in the local party leadership that I was able to meet John F. Kennedy as he set out on his successful campaign for the presidency in the fall of 1959. I was introduced when Senator Kennedy came to a political event at the Westchester Glen Island Casino.

The senator shook my hand and asked me about my work with the labor movement, so I told him about the Ladies' Garment Workers and the garment center rallies. I said, "I'm a big follower of yours. I'm never going to stop working for you." And he told me, "John, keep it up."

His brother Robert, known by everyone as Bobby, was managing his presidential campaign, and he made a strong impression on me too. It was the summer of 1960 and I was president of the 9th Ward Democratic club. An old friend, Ken Brown, was running for the New York State Assembly and had asked me to be his campaign manager. All of the State Assembly and Senate candidates and their campaign managers, including me, were invited to a campaign meeting at the Biltmore Hotel. Bobby Kennedy was the main speaker. Bobby gave a really strong pep talk. He could be so blunt. There was a split at the time within the state party organization. Bobby told us he did not care how we went on that intraparty vote. But he said, "God help you on the day after the election if you weren't with my brother!"

I sat there thinking, "God almighty, are we getting our marching orders!" It made such an impression on me. I told his brother Edward "Ted" Kennedy the story years later, and Teddy laughed. "That's my brother," he said.

President Kennedy's Inspiring Words at Penn South. Of course, John Kennedy won the 1960 presidential election. Two years later, I was fortunate to be in the crowd when he came to Manhattan to dedicate the Penn South Cooperative, a large new housing development for working families that was sponsored by my union, the ILGWU. A lot of prominent people came to the dedication, from Mayor Robert Wagner to Governor Nelson Rockefeller and former First Lady Eleanor Roosevelt. Of course, the ILGWU President David Dubinsky was seated near President Kennedy, and so was AFL-CIO President George Meany.

To be able to see President John F. Kennedy on Seventh Avenue was a real thrill. I know it is not such a big deal to be Catholic in America these days, but back in 1960 it was a huge deal that the president of the United States was a Catholic. Having President Kennedy as a role model, helped Catholic men, women, and children across the nation – including me – feel that we could contribute to our country in a meaningful way without falling under the shadow of discrimination.

That day I heard one of the finest labor union speeches that a U.S president ever delivered. JFK was so inspiring. He talked about unions as a force for change in our society and called on us to do more. "The unfinished business of this country is your business," he told us. I never forgot that.

Little did I imagine that nearly 50 years later, I would be back at Penn South giving a speech myself to celebrate union pension investments that exemplify the commitment to communities that President Kennedy was talking about. But I will get to that later.

Going to Work at Local 32B. In the early 1960s, I took a job as contract director for Local 32B of the Building Service Employees Union. At the time 32B represented male maintenance workers in the real estate industry in Manhattan, Queens, Brooklyn, and Staten Island – the janitors, elevator operators, doormen, and in some cases building superintendents in apartment and office buildings.

David Sullivan, an Irishman from County Cork, was president of the international union, known at the time as the Building Service Employees Union, and later as the Service Employees International Union. He was also the former president of 32B and had recommended me for the job. Sullivan's assistant, Tom Donahue, whom I knew through the Industrial Relations Research Association, had worked for 32B in the past, and he got me together with Sullivan. At the time, Sullivan was interviewing me for a job with the international union. But before we got into the details, in the middle of the interview, he said to Tom, "He might be better here in Local 32B."

So Thomas Shortman, 32B's president, hired me. Tom was from Brooklyn, a diamond in the rough with a real New York vocabulary. He had a great personality and persuasive powers that I've never seen surpassed. And he knew how to use the power that he had to truly represent the workers.

The job was a great opportunity for me because this was a very good time for strengthening representation in the building maintenance industry. In the wave of new construction after World War II, most buildings were organized right after they opened. The maintenance contractors at these buildings were not necessarily out to fight the union off. They realized the importance of maintaining a stable industry, and in many cases, they would transfer workers from an older unionized building into a newly constructed one, to train new employees and to work with the new staff. All of that helped with organizing.

But where you had contractors that did not encourage the unionization of their buildings, our union had to be more aggressive. We had to enlist the support of other unions that did work in the building. In a newly constructed building, the building trades were good supporters, as were the Communications Workers who ran the new phone lines and the Sanitation Workers, too. These were all unions that the employer depended upon to get the building in shape. So, in most cases, the employer kept his hands off and the workers could go through the democratic process of expressing their interest in joining the union.

For me, personally, the new job was an opportunity to do what I most wanted to do – to help make life better for workers at the low end of the wage scale. Without a doubt, working for and with the members of 32B showed me the relevance of the Catholic social teachings I had learned in the classroom. I got so much satisfaction out of being able to help rank-and-file workers through some tough times.

One of my college jobs had been working as a janitor, so I had some experience with hard and dirty low-wage work. But 32B's members were probably the highest paid building service workers, because 32B was a strong and aggressive organization. The union had developed benefit programs that the employers participated in, providing workers good pension and health benefits. Local 32B represented a substantial part of the industry, and that made them strong.

Early Mentors at 32B. Tom Shortman and Dave Sullivan were both charter members of 32B. In fact, almost all of 32B's leadership at the time went back to the days of the 1934 elevator operators' strike that shut down the garment district and built up the union. They knew how to fight aggressively to persuade employers to negotiate a contract. Tom Young, 32B's vice president, who was originally from St. Kitts, would tell stories about how the landlords wanted to wipe the union out, and brought in strikebreakers and goons. It could get bloody, but he said, "We gave as good as we got."

Arthur Harckham, 32B's secretary-treasurer, had stories about battling the mob. In the early days, a couple of guys had showed up outside his home in Long Island and beat the hell out of him and scared his family to death, but he always survived.

Cecil Ward, who had joined 32B in 1935, had a big influence on me. One building manager, who did not like the idea of a black man from Trinidad running elevators, tried to have him fired. So Cecil had turned around and started organizing.

Cecil immediately took me under his wing. He showed me the value of patience, courtesy, dignity, and respect for working men and women – and the value of quiet strength: Cecil Ward could stop a boss in mid-sentence with his steely glare. When he died in 2008, at age 97, he was the last of the generation that had created a union, and a movement, that lifted hundreds of thousands of families out of poverty – the generation that gave me my start at 32B.

8,000 Union Contracts. I fell into line very easily in Local 32B. I really liked the work that I was doing, managing the contract information for every single contract that the local had, and they had over 8,000 contracts. Some, like the contract for Rockefeller Center or the Empire State Building, covered hundreds of workers. Many, many more, like the contracts for tenement walk-ups, covered a single janitor.

Wages for apartments and commercial buildings were essentially set by associations like the Realty Advisory Board, the major coordinating body for real estate that was owner-operated or maintained. The union's officers negotiated the master agreements, which set the model for the other agreements. For instance, the one-person building would have an independent contract that was modeled after what was negotiated with the association. Often I was invited to observe and hear what was being negotiated. That way I understood the background of the points we were pressing. Later on, when I worked with the attorneys on writing the contract, I could make sure that the language really achieved what we said we were looking for in the negotiations.

The various employer associations were responsible for getting their individual members to sign the contract. But with the independents – the small one-person buildings – we had to deal directly with the employer and strike those independent buildings if they refused to sign. That was all supervised from my office.

Meeting George Meany on the Picket Line. Early in my career at Local 32B, I had the privilege of standing side by side with AFL-CIO President George Meany when he came to New York City to join members of his own Plumbers local in their fight for a better contract. On a bitingly cold winter's day, the strikers were marching outside a construction site that happened to be next to the offices of Local 32B on East 35th Street. Some of the leaders from the New York Building Trades were also marching. I made sure our offices were available to assist the striking workers in any way we could, with coffee and sandwiches as well as a place to get a break from the cold. After the picketing finished I had a chance to have a late meal with George Meany. He was very warm and appreciative – the exact opposite of the image of him as a gruff, cigar-chomping labor leader. I was glad that he was able to see that Local 32B was actively on the Plumbers' side.

That day with George Meany provided me with a real sense of what labor solidarity means. I like to think I took this lesson with me as I moved up the ladder in 32B, SEIU, the American labor movement, and throughout my career.

Moving Up in the Local. The longer I worked at 32B, the more confidence President Tom Shortman had in me. More and more he would include me in discussions and meetings.

One memorable example was when Tom asked me to fill in for him when he was unable to attend a dinner with Nelson Rockefeller at the Governor's Mansion in Albany. This was shortly after Rockefeller, a moderate Republican, had been re-elected as governor with our support. Local 32B had a good relationship with the Rockefellers. Rockefeller Center had been built with union construction in the 1930s. Its operation and maintenance workers were organized, and the employers negotiated decent, fair contracts, which were similar to what was negotiated with the Realty Advisory Board. Rockefeller Center was considered a prestigious building service job.

So my wife and I headed up to the dinner in Albany. Our children were very young, and we had to drive up and back the same day. But we had a great time. I knew a lot of the people there, especially the labor folks. I also appreciated the opportunity to develop my relationship with Victor Borella, a Dartmouth classmate of Nelson Rockefeller's, who was responsible for labor relations at Rockefeller Center. He was a very decent employer, and our acquaintance proved helpful over time.

I had a piece of good luck in 1967 when Tom Shortman's assistant, Bill Quirk, decided to take another job, and Tom offered me the position of assistant to the president. It would mean supervising different pieces of organizing, contract negotiations, administrative affairs, and 32B's participation in community affairs and legislative matters. And it created new opportunities for me because in 1968 Tom recommended to the executive board that the assistant to the president be an elected job and treated as a fifth officer. When that was approved by the executive board and at a rank-and-file membership meeting, Tom recommended me for the position, and I was elected.

My predecessor Tom Donahue often would say, "I had the job of assistant to the president at 32B. Quirk had that job. Neither one of us ever had the opportunity to run for elected office. Then along comes this guy Sweeney." But I had hopes that I would have that opportunity.

One of the reasons I was able to run for that office with no opposition was the work I had done on members' grievances when I served as contract director. Some of their hardship stories would really break your heart. If I could get a guy his job back, or if I could get him another job, or if I could get his pay corrected to the right salary, I felt good about it, and I built a great relationship. The members knew I was working for them.

Becoming Secretary-Treasurer of 32B. The other officers really respected me and I had developed a good relationship with them. But they all would have liked to succeed Tom Shortman, and so they kept an eye on me. I say that in a nice way because they were always helpful to me and, like Tom, they respected the work that I could do.

When Tom Shortman died in 1972, Arthur Harckham exercised his rights as secretary-treasurer, and he was elected to fill the vacancy of the president. Dick Cancellere, the secretary (and another 32B charter member), was elected as secretary-treasurer, and then he unexpectedly developed cancer and died.

I talked to Arthur about the opportunity to become secretary-treasurer, but he said, "Who's going to handle that job?" pointing to the office next to his that I was in.

I said, "Oh, I'll try to do both. I will do both." And I did. I became secretary-treasurer in 1973, and I did not neglect the president in any way. I was writing remarks or providing talking points for different events, and I was supervising staff.

Clerical workers at 32B were members of OPEIU, the Office and Professional Employees International Union. Now it was my job to handle wage negotiations and other contract issues. That was one of the toughest adjustments for me – negotiating with the union and meeting with workers with whom I was very friendly. I would say, "I want you to get as much as we possibly can justify." That still did not stop them from fighting back.

Getting Active Beyond the Local Union. By this time I was getting more active in the international union, which had changed its name in 1968 from the Building Service Employees Union to the Service Employees International Union. Under its new president, George Hardy, SEIU was making a real effort to broaden its membership base. In 1972 I joined SEIU's executive board, and in 1973 I became an international vice president of the union. This was around the time that SEIU was pressing Congress to extend the National Labor Relations Act to cover employees of nonprofit hospitals and state and local government, industries in which SEIU was actively organizing members. There was a new spirit of action in the international union and I wanted to be a part of it.

This movement at the top encouraged me to broaden Local 32B's reach, especially in legislative matters. On the West Coast, for example, there were a California State Council and a Western Regional Council. These councils were developed by George Hardy before he became president of SEIU. The state council was primarily a legislative body, whose members would lobby the state capital for legislation important to service employees and make endorsements of candidates based on their legislative record. The regional council followed the lead of the national union in supporting legislation in a particular state or region.

We followed the model of the West Coast structure to form the New York State Council, which started out as a legislative committee. But then I worked with Arthur Harckham to formalize it into a council, with a constitution and resources from SEIU's per capita tax. It became very effective and developed a strong grassroots mobilization that strengthened the focus of SEIU's local unions on state politics and got out the vote. We built on the political work that had gone on in SEIU's local joint councils, and we just spread it throughout the region. We always had a strong concern for health care, for example, and for occupational safety and health, free time, and job security. Those were the kinds of issues that we encouraged our local union leadership to actively support at the grassroots level. With support from the national union, the state council also ran educational programs for local union officers and staff who were working directly on political or legislative activity and organizing.

With that council underway, I helped organize the SEIU Eastern Regional Conference, working with an SEIU leader from upstate New York, Walter Butler. It was 1975, and the economy was in a deep recession. Our plan was to aggressively promote organizing and political action to help SEIU members from Maine to Florida, as well as unorganized workers in the region, to fight the recession. This was pretty effective because we had a national union that was getting more aggressive in these areas, without taking over from the local unions or joint councils, but strengthening them in all of this work.

My Election as 32B's President. Around this time, Arthur Harckham, the president of 32B, was seriously ill. I kept in close touch with him and tried to make sure that whatever we were doing was cleared by him. Finally, I broached the subject of his retirement, and he did not balk at the idea. But he was frank and said he had really hoped to be able to work longer. I was ready for that kind of a discussion. I told him, "You can retire and you can be emeritus, and you can continue to have responsibilities. You can work that out with the other officers, and we can make a recommendation to the executive board." He was very active in the Central Labor Council, so I made sure that he could continue there, and I told him he could remain on the executive board of SEIU until the end of his term. That seemed to be acceptable to him.

Arthur made the recommendation to the executive board that I succeed him as president, and at the next executive board meeting it was on the agenda to be discussed. Tom Young, the vice president, was interested but, given his age, he did not push. In the end, I had no opposition. In fact, when I was elected president at a membership meeting in February 1976, Tom placed my name in nomination.

"I have worked hard, but I have been well trained," I told the members who had just elected me. But I also told them that it was time for new thinking, new planning, and new action, because it was a pretty challenging moment. New York City was almost bankrupt. This was around the time that President Gerald Ford rejected a federal bailout for the city, and the New York *Daily News* printed the headline "Ford to City: Drop Dead." We were also on the brink of negotiating a new apartment house agreement with the Real Estate Advisory Board.

But having had the experience that I did as an assistant to Tom Shortman and having been through prior negotiations, I was prepared. I had established relationships with the employer representatives as well as our own leadership and the politicians in the city. And I knew the union so well. I knew what the benefits package encompassed and what the membership would need to see in a new contract to ratify it. I was pretty confident that, with a little strike once in a while, I would be able to negotiate decent contracts.

Launching a Surprise Strike. In April 1976, just two months after I was elected president of 32B, I was facing the possibility of a major citywide strike. The Realty Advisory Board was looking for major concessions from the union in our next contract. They wanted to cut wages 10 percent, eliminate the cost-of-living clause, and reduce sick leave and holidays. These would be the first concessions in 32B's history – and that was not going to happen on my watch.

Instead, the union was looking for a $50 a week wage increase, a better cost-of-living provision, a 35-hour week, and improved health, welfare, and pension benefits. So the two sides were pretty far apart. A couple of weeks in, the Realty Advisory Board dropped their wage cut demands but they still wanted to cut benefits, so we were basically deadlocked. The employers wanted to use us as pawns in the rent-control debate. That was a complicated issue because on the one hand, we understood the landlords' need to raise rents in order to perform necessary repairs; on the other hand, many of our members lived in rent-controlled apartments. I think the Realty Advisory Board was hoping that if they drew out the negotiations, the governor or the mayor or somebody would come up with a recommendation that would address the rent-control issue. But I decided that we had gone far enough, and whatever they were able to get on rent control would be up to them.

I brought 32B's officers, the executive board, and the strike committee into the office on a Sunday and expressed how serious I thought the situation was. I said, "I'd like to recommend that we go on strike." I had it all set up in terms of how we would start and what we would do to build up support among the members. I sent the organizers and executive board and the strike committee out into the field. They went around, especially to the big buildings, and called together the employees to tell them that the negotiations really were not going well and that we would have to think of taking some strong action.

The members were ready for it. We decided that the time was now. We told them all to come back in at five o'clock the next morning and to be prepared to go out on strike, with picket signs and all the rest.

The owners woke up the next morning with the radio and newspapers declaring that there was a strike. Ed Sulzberger was the chair of our Realty Advisory Board committee. He said, "This is like a Pearl Harbor that Sweeney pulled on us." Well, I could not have thought of a better expression to use. A lot of these buildings were luxury residences, so the last thing in the world that these condo and co-op owners and high-paying renters wanted was to be inconvenienced by a strike.

Running a strike yourself is an awesome responsibility. You say your prayers that you are going to be successful in helping these workers achieve some greater dignity, because you are taking a risk. But I had an optimistic feeling that we had done everything possible in trying to negotiate a contract, and this was a last resort. I always say – I said it then, I say it now – the threat of a strike can be very powerful.

I think it really shocked them, because even their lawyers could not believe that I would pull a strike like this. Little did they know...

Garbage Crisis. Abraham "Abe" Beame was the mayor of New York and invited me to come down to City Hall and meet with him about the strike. He and I had a decent relationship. He was under a lot of pressure about the strike because it was May and it was a very warm springtime. The sanitation workers – members of the Uniformed Sanitationmen's Association, a Teamsters local – were honoring our picket lines. They were not picking up the garbage at buildings where our workers were on strike. With the heat, the garbage was beginning to smell, the newspaper pile-up was getting critical, and tenants were complaining.

I said, "Mr. Mayor, these Teamsters are not picking up the garbage, because they feel very strongly that these building service workers deserve a contract and deserve a decent wage increase. The building service workers would feel the same way if the Teamsters were out on strike."

He said, "Can't you call DeLury and ask him to start picking up the garbage?" John DeLury was the head of the Uniformed Sanitationmen's Association.

I said, "I can try. I don't know if he can tell his members to cross a picket line."

Then the mayor said, "If I call him, will you get on?"

I said, "Sure. I want to get this resolved as much as you do. The real culprits here are the owners."

Mayor Beame got his secretary to call John DeLury. As I recall, the mayor said to him: "John, I have Sweeney here, trying to find a way to get this strike settled. I'm getting beat up all over the place, the newspapers and tenants and everybody. Is there some way that your members could pick up the garbage?"

DeLury told him, "If Sweeney would tell us that he wants us to pick up the garbage, I could tell my members that he's saying that, but I don't know if they'll do this."

"So can I put him on?" the mayor asked.

DeLury said, "Hi, John. Getting tough, huh?"

I said, "Yeah, it is, but thank you very much for the support that your members are giving us. We know how strongly they feel and how they relate to these workers. They see them a couple of times a week."

He said, "I understand, and I understand what you're up against, but you don't have to tell me any more. I'll talk to my men."

I knew that he was going to continue to support the building service workers, so I said, "Is there anything more, Mr. Mayor, you want to say?"

"No, that's okay."

The mayor said to me, "I don't understand this. I appointed his son a judge."

I said, "Oh, Mr. Mayor. This has nothing to do with that. The son was a good appointment but John DeLury wants to do the right thing here. He's elected by his members and he has to have some democracy in the organization as to what the members want him to do."

Needless to say, the garbage did not get picked up.

Resolving the Strike. Harry Van Arsdale, Jr., the head of the New York City Central Labor Council, also supported us all the way. Harry was a trade unionist through and through. An Electrical Worker by training, he was the longtime leader of Local 3, the largest local of the International Brotherhood of Electrical Workers, and he had a well-earned reputation for organizing workers that people said could not be organized, like taxi drivers and hospital workers. He also had very strong political connections that helped him work behind the scenes on many labor issues. Harry was the kind of leader that kept New York City a strong union town. I had developed a good working relationship with him and also a good friendship. He was the closest I could see to being a statesman on behalf of labor.

Harry knew that I was going to meet with Abe Beame and that there was going to be a mediation session, and he was very interested in the outcome. When I got home very late that night, and Maureen told me Harry had called. "He was anxious to know how you made out in mediation and said that you should call him, no matter what time you get in."

I said, "I'm not going to call anybody at two o'clock in the morning."

At six o'clock the next morning, the phone rang. "John, I told Maureen to have you call me whenever you got home."

I told him I thought we had made some progress but still had to keep at it. I said the mayor really wanted to get this resolved. Harry wanted me to let him know if there were any new developments he should know about.

And he did get involved. He went to some people in the real estate industry like Rex Tompkins, a powerful figure in the industry, one of the Realty Advisory Board's representatives. Harry urged him to separate the contract negotiations from the rent-freeze fight. Then the *New York Times* made the same point in an editorial in support of the union and the workers. In any event, Harry stayed with us until we finally got it resolved – which we did a few days later.

The 1976 apartment strike was the longest, largest, and toughest strike in 32B's history. Overall it was a victory. After 17 days that disrupted services to tenants in luxury buildings and inconvenienced the public, we negotiated a $35 raise over three years, an improved cost-of-living clause, and preservation of our benefits. But just as important, the strike let our employers know, in no uncertain terms, that 32B was strong and united and that the members were not going to watch the hard-won gains of the past be wiped out. We fought hard and played fair and stayed true to our union values. And we built a stronger union as a result.

Creating SEIU's Largest Local. Right around the time that Local 32B elected me president, another building service union, Local 32J, was really stirring things up in New York. Local 32J, first organized in 1936, represented the women who cleaned offices; they used to call them charwomen. These women's pay and benefits were inferior to those of the men in 32B.

Most of the women in 32J worked at night, from five o'clock in the evening until ten. They were mostly immigrant workers, often from Eastern Europe. When 32J sent a notice out to their members, they put it in about five or six different languages. They had initiated all kinds of projects, like a safety program for the women going home at night.

Local 32J's members worked in many of the same buildings as 32B's, and they might work for the same contractor. But because their jobs were defined as women's work versus men's work, their pay scales were lower. Men generally worked in public areas like the lobby or by the elevators, all the way up the building; the women would be inside cleaning the private offices. The location made all the difference, so a male member of 32B cleaning one side of a glass door in a public hallway would earn more than a woman cleaning the other side of the door in a private office.

Cleaning workers belonging to Locals 32B and 32J demonstrate in New York City in 1975, two years before we merged the two locals.

After the Equal Pay Act of 1963, 32J's members started protesting this arrangement. They began bringing class action suits against the contractors and building owners, and in 1976 the U.S. Department of Labor and the Equal Employment Opportunity Commission approved consent decrees that established their right to equal pay with men. Now the leaders of 32J wanted to equalize the women's pay with 32B's significantly higher wage rate. And they wanted to improve the benefits. Since Local

32J and Local 32B bargained with many of the same contractors, the idea of merging the unions – and their pension and health and welfare funds – made a lot of sense. Both locals would be stronger if there was only one set of negotiations.

We eventually merged the two local unions in 1977. I had the support of the 32J people, particularly Joe Bauman, who was president at the time. I gave them my word that as union officer positions became vacant for whatever reason, 32J's officers would be given consideration for the move up. So it fell into place. Joe Bauman became a vice president of the merged local, which was called Local 32B-32J at the time (now SEIU 32BJ). The secretary-treasurer of 32J became an assistant secretary-treasurer. Members came to the 32B-32J local membership meetings, and the organizing staff all became organizers of 32B-32J.

With some attention to the transition, we were able to make a very good merger. And with more than 46,000 members now, Local 32B-32J became the SEIU's largest local, with real clout.

On Strike at the World Trade Center. Early in 1978, the newly merged union was tested at the World Trade Center. We had hundreds of workers employed there under a contract with TEMCO, a well-known company that had held the building service contract since 1970. The Port Authority, which owned the World Trade Center, decided to bring in a new contractor, and the new contractor decided to get rid of the TEMCO workers. They not only wanted to cut the workforce, but any workers they hired back would be considered new workers and paid the minimum wage. So after 32B-32J members refused a wage cut, a reduction of hours, and a loss of seniority and benefits, the new contractor brought in nonunion workers to do the job. Essentially, the former TEMCO workers were locked out. We struck.

The World Trade Center concourse provided public access to the subway and a shopping mall. It was February and bitter cold, so we set up pickets inside the building. We held demonstrations in the middle of the day, when area workers were all going to lunch. There was always a crowd.

One day we decided to have a rally inside. We started this around eleven-thirty. By twelve-thirty you could hardly move, it was so crowded. We were orderly but the police were on hand to make sure that we behaved ourselves. I could see the lawyers for the Port Authority in the back of this crowd; they were just looking to see if they could find a reason to go after us. They allowed us to speak into a bullhorn, and we explained that the employer threw the former employees out, brought in inexperienced workers, and really did not want to pay decent wages. Somebody had a firecracker or smoke bomb. People moved on. But it was an action that got a lot of press, and it succeeded in getting the Port Authority involved in negotiations with us.

Outreach to Domestic and Home Health Workers. Because of what I remembered about my mother's work situation, I always had the dream that I could organize the domestic workers. I thought 32B's members, especially those employed in the luxury apartment buildings, could help. We represented the doormen, who were friendly with the workers coming in to clean apartments. I started searching around to see what organizations might be looking after these domestic workers. I found an organization that was mostly African American women, the Professional Household Workers Association. It was a very loosely knit organization headed up by Benjamin McLaurin, a former officer of the Sleeping Car Porters. I admired how he had worked so hard with these folks with few resources.

I met with a committee of these household workers and talked to them about what we could do to strengthen their organization and help them with organizing. I also asked Cecil Ward, who was now a vice president of 32B-32J, to work on this. McLaurin was very upbeat. He saw the potential.

We called our group the Household Workers Organizing Committee, and by 1978 Cecil had a staff of four organizers on the case. He would fire up these workers by saying things like, "We are on the march to organize and free you good women from slavery." There was even a rally at City Hall with union signs saying, "Take us out of slavery."

We concentrated on women employed by contracting firms, because Hugh Carey, New York's governor, had signed a bill in 1976 giving them the right to organize. And we had our first victory in 1978 when 150 mostly Chinese housekeepers, homemakers, and home attendants employed by the First Chinese Presbyterian Church voted to join 32B-32J.

Around this time a lot of the same domestic workers were looking to do home health care work. The city and state were involved with home health care and there was funding for these workers. Local 1199, the National Union of Hospital and Health Care Employees in New York City, was already organizing these workers, but not successfully enough, as far as I could see. I convinced Peter Ottley, who headed SEIU's Hotel Workers union, Local 144, to join me, and together we created an entity called 144-32B-32J and began organizing. But I recognized that competing with 1199 was not going to be productive. I talked with Ottley and with my old friend Leon Davis, the longtime leader of 1199, about forming one union. As it turned out, the members chose to go with 1199, and that is where they are today.

I really never had much time for local leaders of any union who ignored organizing opportunities and then complained when others stepped in, saying that "he doesn't belong" or "it's not really his industry." I said then, when we were fighting over home health care workers, and I say now, "You're wrong. If you aren't out there organizing, other guys have every right to go out and match you and organize new workers. And shame on you for criticizing them."

Meeting of the SEIU executive board December 1979. Pictured with SEIU's president George Hardy (center) and board member Walter Butler.

3

BUILDING THE SUPER UNION: MOVING
UP TO SEIU'S PRESIDENCY

Right before Christmas, in 1979, I got some shocking news that would change my life. George Hardy, SEIU's president, called me at about three in the morning and told me that the union's secretary-treasurer, Tony Weinlein, had died. Tony had joined the SEIU in the 1940s, and he was the research director for years before becoming SEIU's secretary-treasurer in 1976. I really was taken aback. George told me that Tony had been at home with his family, playing the piano and singing Christmas carols – he was a great pianist – and he keeled over at the piano, apparently from a heart attack.

George said, "I want to recommend to the board that you succeed him to fill the vacancy." I was still stunned and asked for a little time to think about this. "What the hell do you need time for?" he said. We agreed that I would call him back in two hours. When he called the board on the death, he wanted to be able to recommend me for the position.

I talked to my wife, Maureen. Politically I was in good shape. The 32B-32J merger transition was going well. Our children, Trish and John, were young and we would have to relocate to Washington, but I said for a while I would try to commute back and forth. So Maureen finally agreed, and I called George Hardy. I told him that I would probably have to commute initially. He said, "I don't care what the hell you do." That was the way he was, and he knew himself that he did not give up his local in California for a while after he was first elected president, in order to make sure he had a handle on the union out there.

So I took the job of secretary-treasurer at SEIU. But I kept my hand in at 32B-32J because I wanted to make sure that we had a strong transition. We were on a roll, we had good organizing programs, we had done well with the 32J merger, but it would require continued work to reassure the members of 32J that we were going to do as good a job, if not better, on their issues. [1]

It was a bit of a grind for me. I would go into the local on Monday morning and I would fly down to Washington on Tuesday morning on the first shuttle. Then I would fly back on Thursday night on the last shuttle, and I went to the local on Friday and Saturday. I took Sundays off. That worked fine for a while, but it was grueling and I knew that I could not keep it up.

Eyeing SEIU's Presidency. When George Hardy called me the night that Tony Weinlein died, I knew that becoming secretary-treasurer would bring me closer to the presidency of SEIU. What I did not know was how close.

We all knew that Hardy was planning to retire; the question was, who was going to succeed him? Dick Cordtz, a longtime organizer and president of the union's Central States Conference, really wanted the job and assumed that he would have Hardy's support. But my moving into the secretary-treasurer spot really shook him up, and he was looking for a commitment from me to let him be president for just one term. I knew those kinds of deals do not usually work out, so I told him, "I have the support of a lot of people, and I'm really going to pursue this." I encouraged him to think about the second spot, secretary-treasurer. I recognized that Dick had worked very hard for SEIU, but I persisted.

Whenever I had the opportunity to move up, I always consulted with people that I respected, and I tried to be as low-key about it as possible. I never had anyone that I highly respected tell me not to do it or that it was the wrong time, and that meant something to me. I certainly took advantage of timing. Had I backed off, I might not have gotten the opportunity again, or I might have had to fight very, very hard to get it. But when I knew I had the support of the majority of people, especially those whom I respected, I usually took advantage of it.

I also knew that if I decided to continue in the secretary-treasurer spot, George Hardy would resent my not taking advantage of the opportunity he was creating for me, and I hope he thought that I would be the better choice of the two. Dick could be very aggressive in dealing with people, and my personality was different. That was why I think he decided to back me.

Celebrating the 1978 organizing victory of the N.Y. State Public Employees Federation, with SEIU's organizing director John Geagan, AFT president Al Shanker, SEIU VP Cecil Ward, and SEIU field rep John Kraemer.

The fact is, I wanted to be president, and I had worked pretty hard to get myself ready for the job. I had worked my ass off. When I was at 32B, I was proud of who I represented and what I was able to do. In the joint council I had worked with every local and supported whatever their needs were in negotiations. I went to their rank-and-file membership meetings when I could. When I was head of the Eastern Conference, I was up and down the East Coast, going to conferences and meetings and running organizing sessions as well as political sessions in different locals in different states. That was how I got to know people in different states. I also worked with other affiliates and had great relationships with Al Shanker, the president of the American Federation of Teachers; with Victor Gottbaum, president of New York's largest municipal union, District Council 37 of AFSCME, the American Federation of State, County and Municipal Employees; and with Leon Davis, the founder of District 1199, the National Union of Health Care Workers. So I had done my homework.

Election as SEIU President. And then came the election. My election at the 1980 SEIU convention was no contest. Dick Cordtz had finally come around and run for secretary-treasurer. As it turned out, Dick and I really worked very well together. He proved to be a loyal, trusted, and effective partner.

When I made my acceptance speech at the 1980 convention I promised that SEIU would continue to advance, to expand, to lead the good fight for human dignity and decency. And I thought I had a good chance to keep that promise, because what I brought to the job as president was a new openness to the management of the organization, as well as a focus on creative organizing tactics.

Pussycat or Boat Rocker? George Hardy was a tough act to follow as president of SEIU. George was a very outspoken person. He had quite a reputation for shaking things up. Once when he was at a meeting at the White

House, he let President Gerald Ford know that just a few blocks away, "these damn employers" were paying janitors "a lousy 10 cent increase, . . . and who the hell could live on that?"

So when I was elected to succeed him, Abe Raskin, the *New York Times* labor editor, wondered whether Hardy's retirement signaled "a slump back to pussycat tameness" for the SEIU. Abe wrote that I was as quiet and polite as Hardy was "rambunctious" and that I looked more like a "bookish cleric" than a boat rocker. When Abe asked me whether I shared Hardy's view that big corporations were ruling and ruining the country, he seemed a little surprised when I said, "Most of us do."

George Hardy's real strength had been in organizing. He worked at it himself and actually ran organizing conferences all across the country for our local unions. His motto was, "If they're breathing, organize them." He also encouraged mergers, especially with independent public employee unions. He brought in John Geagan, our organizing director in those days, from his operation in California. George was equally strong when it came to research. He started a program of placing people in different states with the job title of research specialist. The research program went far beyond the usual preparation for negotiations, but involved planning for organizing campaigns and also helping with state and city legislative work.

I intended to build upon those programs George started, to keep the SEIU growing. It would not be easy, though, because by 1980 a conservative tide was sweeping the nation. Right-to-work campaigns were taking direct aim at the trade union movement, and tax-cutting measures like California's Proposition 13 threatened the livelihoods of thousands of public employees. Under George Hardy's leadership, the SEIU had grown from 430,000 members in 1971 to 650,000 in 1980, and service worker wages had doubled, at least. But in 1980, George and I both knew that there were great challenges ahead. In Ronald Reagan's America, we would have to double our efforts just to stand still.

A New Structure to Mobilize the Rank-and-File. My agenda as president of SEIU was to respect the needs of workers as strongly as I could. I thought it was important for the union to grow, but I also thought that it was important to have strong relationships with rank-and-file workers, respecting their ideas, their needs, and to mobilize workers around legislative and political issues. I recognized that we could continue to grow, and grow a lot. But if we were not able to change government policies and shape legislation that was critical to rank-and-file workers and their right to organize, we would be a failure.

My first goal as president was to restructure the organization. Because of my work with the international union, I really had a great appreciation for its staff. But as a result of what I heard during the campaign in terms of suggestions from different leaders around the country, I thought that we could develop a more effective way of running the international union and servicing the local unions. This became one of my major goals.

In June 1982 the SEIU executive board approved my restructuring plan. Existing departments were reorganized to centralize aid to local unions and councils, and new departments including Education, Civil Rights, and Organization and Field Services were set up. The last one, Organization and Field Services, was designed to help local unions develop strategies to fight anti-union policies. Regional offices were opened up to bring the international union's resources closer to the struggle. With these changes, people began to think differently about the benefits of an international union and the support it could provide.

Fostering Pride in Each Industry Within SEIU. At the same time, my experience on the local level got me thinking about a new divisional structure for SEIU. At 32B, the largest local union in SEIU at the time, I had worked to pursue a building service agenda, organize more aggressively, bring 32B and 32J together, and strengthen their focus on legislative issues that affected their members' interests as private sector workers. I thought that this approach could be developed in other industries served by SEIU. Having locals in the same industry talk to each other and mobilize around the issues important to them, whether they worked in the public sector, in retail, or in health care, would surely help us when new organizing opportunities arose.

We represented workers in so many different sectors that I saw it was important to promote a sense of pride in each industry and to structure the SEIU in such a way that each industry could get the most out of its affiliation with the international. So in 1984, we established new divisions for the major SEIU industries – health care, building service, public sector, clerical, and jewelry, gas, and industrial. The point was to bring the leadership of each industry group together, so that they could learn from each other and work together to promote their common interests.

When we created the Public Employee Division in SEIU, for instance, it gave the public employees' locals a sense of their own group, their own organizing person, their own research, and all of the things that were important to them. These new divisions – chaired by a local union president or state organization president – also gave us the opportunity to develop a new level of leadership and a new level of experience.

To get all this done, I needed a good team with me in the union's executive office. Bob Welsh became my chief of staff. He had held the same position with my predecessor, George Hardy. He actually remained with me for the next 37 years, eventually coming with me to the AFL-CIO. Bob was an excellent architect for building a modern, effective organization at SEIU and later at the AFL-CIO. We had a lot in common, particularly our shared interest in the teachings of our Catholic faith as it relates to civil rights and community work.

Diversifying SEIU's Leadership. In the 1980s we were not only restructuring SEIU, we were changing the face of union leadership: Some of SEIU's newest leaders were young and many were female, including Rosemary Trump, SEIU's first female vice president, who was elected with me in 1980. She made "women's issues" – pay equity, support for equal rights – part of the SEIU agenda. That was a very big deal at the time.

Four years later, Ophelia McFadden, the union's first female African American vice president, was elected to head our Public Employee Division. Ophelia was a good trade unionist and a tough taskmaster who had no problem telling me what was on her mind, in a nice way. She was an important leader for us, as she was well connected with the civil rights organizations and had really good relationships with California leaders such as Governor "Pat" Brown, his son (and future governor) Jerry, and Congresswoman Maxine Waters. That really mattered to public employees, whose bosses are either elected officials or political appointees.

At the same time, we were bringing on new young organizers who came out of the anti-war movement, the civil rights movement, and the women's rights movement – another move that seemed revolutionary to some of my fellow union leaders. But that did not bother me. The effort to restructure the union was really part of a mosaic of change that brought in lots of new blood and lots of new leadership, which was just what we needed in the 1980s. I was proud that SEIU was leading the way.

Organizing the Pink Collar Workforce. Right around the time I came in as SEIU president, people were starting to talk about the new service economy. Service industries employed a majority of the American workforce in the 1980s, and many of those workers were women. But you could not tell that from looking at the labor movement. So we had the challenge to organize new groups of service workers. To do that, we had to identify the issues that mattered to these workers and persuade them that SEIU could help.

In 1981 we chartered a new arm of SEIU, District 925, as part a national campaign to organize office workers – what we called the pink collar workforce. Karen Nussbaum and Jackie Ruff had been organizing these workers since the 1970s, so they had been working for years on issues like pay equity, office automation, day care, career ladders for women, family and medical leave – issues that were not usually a priority for male workers. Karen and Jackie realized that many of these issues could be addressed and resolved through unionization and collective bargaining. While they wanted to keep their public organization, Working Women (later known as 9to5, the National Association of Working Women), they were also willing to join SEIU as District 925 and build a new kind of union based on women and their issues. I saw great potential in these young women and saw that they represented a great opportunity, both for office workers and for SEIU.

The first big campaign with District 925 was against the Equitable Life Assurance Society, and it was a very early and really unsophisticated example of what we now call corporate campaigns. It started out with around 50 office workers in Syracuse who were eager to organize a union, and Walter Butler, SEIU's eastern regional head, was all for moving forward. This was around the time of Jane Fonda's movie, *9 to 5*, which was based on actual stories from Working Women members. Karen and Jane were good friends, and Jane was more than willing to help. We got lots of free publicity, and the momentum seemed to be going our way.

But this was also around the time that President Reagan broke the Air Traffic Controllers' strike, as I will talk about shortly. His actions really cleared the way for anti-union employers to do whatever it took to block organizing efforts. So while the Syracuse office workers' union was certified in 1982, negotiating a contract was another story. Equitable Life showed us what union-busting was all about. The company not only refused to talk to us, they hired a so-called "management" firm to discourage Equitable Life's

10,000 other employees from supporting District 925. But 925 did not back down. We had a big public campaign against Equitable, we called on other unions to boycott the company, and we picketed.

Hundreds and hundreds of workers turned out for a huge demonstration at the Equitable Life building in New York City. I would safely say that the office workers there were in the minority. Maintenance workers, construction workers, they were from all different classifications of work but they understood why these office workers were trying to organize. They wanted them to be successful, and I think that had a very positive impact on SEIU as well as the broader labor community.

It took three years of putting the company in the spotlight to negotiate a union contract – the first one in Equitable Life's history. The contract covered issues of concern to office workers, like automation and video display terminals. As it turned out, though, at the first opportunity the company shut that Syracuse office down. So the campaign proved to be important primarily as a demonstration of SEIU's commitment to organizing women on their own terms, in their own unions, with their own leaders.

That commitment meant a lot to the women who headed independent public employee unions that we were trying to affiliate in the 1980s. Frankly, many of them wanted nothing to do with an AFL-CIO union. But SEIU's support of District 925 was one of the reasons that the clerical bargaining unit of the California State Employees Association – with 30,000 members – voted to join SEIU. Trust is a major issue in merging unions, and our work with District 925 persuaded these workers that they could trust us.

Affiliations with Independent Unions. During George Hardy's time as SEIU president, I had worked with him to build relationships with independent unions and encourage them to affiliate with SEIU. I helped him bring in the Jewelry Workers as an affiliate in 1980; and I helped structure a partnership with the American Federation of Teachers that allowed the New York State Public Employees Federation to affiliate with both unions – that was a job and a half! So I continued to seek opportunities to bring in new affiliates when I became president of SEIU.

Since independent unions often found themselves competing with larger unions to represent public employees, the main draw for affiliating with SEIU was probably the protection offered by Article XX of the AFL-CIO's constitution, which prohibited one AFL-CIO affiliate from raiding another's members.

Public employees in schools, courthouses, libraries, hospitals, and state universities have a long history with SEIU. In the early days, though, public sector workers could not do much more than lobby public officials to improve civil service laws. In fact, although federal workers gained the right to bargain in the early 1960s, it was not until the late '60s and 1970s that state and local workers gained collective bargaining rights. At that point, things began to change – for the better. As the number of government workers increased, attitudes and state laws began to change, and SEIU stepped up its efforts to represent these workers. To keep up with the new organizing opportunities, the union recruited two young leaders from the Pennsylvania Social Services Union, Andy Stern and Anna Burger. Both proved to be key staff: Andy became the Organizing Director and Anna became the National Director of Field Operations.

SEIU had resources that were attractive to public employees. In California, we led the fight against the tax revolt known as Proposition 13, which cut jobs and services, and when we lost that fight in 1979, we helped launch Citizens for Tax Justice, a think-tank that aimed to close corporate tax loopholes and make the wealthy pay their fair share. We had better luck in New York, where we worked hard to pass an agency shop law in 1977. That effort certainly helped us reach an agreement with the New York State Public Employees Federation in 1979. And our record kept improving. By

1980, 20 formerly independent associations, including the Oregon Public Employees Union with 17,000 members, had affiliated with us.

Courting NAGE's Government Employees. Our successes with these public employee groups got the attention of some of the bigger independents, like the National Association of Government Employees, or NAGE. Although for years they had almost shunned the AFL-CIO, now they were getting interested in what an affiliation with an AFL-CIO union could do for them. Originally created in the 1940s as an association to protect the rights of veterans in government employment, NAGE became a labor union during the Kennedy administration when it looked like federal employees were going to get collective bargaining rights. Ken Lyons, who worked at Massachusetts' Charlestown Navy Yard before and after his service in World War II, put the association together.

Ken focused on New England where he worked to organize public employees, and police officers in particular. Soon he found that he was competing with other independent organizations as well as AFL-CIO unions like AFSCME. Ken had developed strong political relationships with Massachusetts political figures such as Congressman Thomas P. "Tip" O'Neill and Congressman John Moakley. He was determined, he was blunt, and he had a lot of style. Ken Lyons was going to build up his union one way or another – and sometimes that meant raiding another union's membership.

In fact he was trying to raid an SEIU local in Massachusetts when the question of affiliating with us came up. Ed Sullivan, our vice president in New England, persuaded him that raiding was too expensive for everybody, and that got the conversation started. Ken called me when he was going to be in Washington and invited me for breakfast. We met and had a very friendly conversation about family and those kinds of things. Then he told me he was considering affiliating with an AFL-CIO union, and said he would like to talk about the possibility of affiliating with SEIU. I followed up by inviting Ken to some of our events, including an eastern regional conference where he met all the SEIU leadership. Of course, he went to some of the other unions to see what they could offer, but he kept coming back to me. I think he trusted me and liked my approach. I was very respectful about telling him that I knew he had good political contacts and that he had a good legislative staff.

Before too long I had convinced Ken that we could fulfill NAGE's needs. But he was a character. I always gave new affiliates a lot of attention. Well, I never gave anyone more attention than I gave Ken Lyons. And it paid off because he became a stronger affiliate, and as his union grew, so did SEIU. When the merger agreement was signed early in 1983, NAGE Local 5000 made SEIU the largest union in New England.

Becoming California's Largest Union. I had a pretty good track record on mergers, probably because I never pushed people or tried to rope them in. The time was right, as far as I was concerned, when people came to me. Our biggest coup was the California State Employees Association, or CSEA, the largest independent civil service union in the country. When it was organized in 1931, state workers were trying to secure pensions. Even though the CSEA did not gain bargaining rights until 1979, the union developed a pretty sophisticated program to educate taxpayers and legislators on the need to improve conditions for state employees.

Around 1983, CSEA began to consider merging with an AFL-CIO union to strengthen its political muscle. Constant competition from larger unions, eager to get CSEA decertified and take its members, was getting expensive, so the leadership sought the protection of the AFL-CIO and its Article XX "no raiding" policy. With that and the growing threat from radical anti-tax efforts to cut government jobs and benefits, the time seemed right for CSEA to join the mainstream labor movement.

It was not an easy sell, though. It took about a year and a half for CSEA's membership to agree to consider the possibility of a merger, and then the question was: Which AFL-CIO union offered CSEA's members the best fit? SEIU was very interested, of course, but so were AFSCME, the International Union of Operating Engineers, the Communications Workers of America, and the United Auto Workers. So we had to show them that, no matter what the other unions said they could do for the membership, SEIU could do it better.

We had some pretty strong assets going in. I was an AFL-CIO vice president, where I was able to advocate on behalf of SEIU, and I was very active in the AFL-CIO's Public Employee Department – in fact, I was executive vice president for state and local government workers. And of course, AFL-CIO Secretary-Treasurer Tom Donahue, with his long history with SEIU, was a tremendous asset since he was in a position to safeguard the integrity of Article XX.

At the 1980 SEIU convention I was photographed as the union's new president with (from left) AFL-CIO secretary-treasurer Tom Donahue; SEIU secretary-treasurer Richard Cordtz; and retiring president George Hardy.

We worked hard to put our best face forward. The CSEA leadership came to Washington, D.C., to spend a day with each of the competing unions, so the race was on to be the first to see them. The day before any meetings were scheduled, we gave them the opportunity to tour the city and meet their senators or members of Congress. People love to go on a tour of the Capitol – I love it myself. We had a nice dinner that evening, and even got them tickets to the Redskins-49ers game, which really broke the ice.

But even if they enjoyed our hospitality, Chuck Valdes, the CSEA leader who was handling the merger on their side, made it very clear that CSEA did not want a guy in Washington telling them what to do. So we gave them the opportunity to talk to our large affiliates and hear how they felt about the international union. I think it was very convincing.

What we proposed was a partnership, rather than a merger: a contractual affiliation that insured CSEA's independence, provided the full protection of Article XX, and allowed CSEA to play a major role in the SEIU's Public Employee Division where it would benefit from the many professional services we offered. We also made sure they understood that this affiliation would make us the largest AFL-CIO union in California and a force so powerful that no one could ignore us.

We must have been pretty persuasive because in January 1984 we completed negotiations and CSEA – which represented 100,000 employees of the State of California, the University of California, and the California State University system – became a full-fledged member of SEIU.

I was really proud of that agreement and of the relationship with CSEA's leaders that grew over the six-month decision-making process, especially when I heard what one of those leaders told reporters about why they chose to join us. The other unions they considered were certainly excellent, this leader said, but CSEA's members felt most comfortable with the style of leadership SEIU offered. I think they felt the same way long after the agreement was signed because we honored our commitments and provided the services we had promised.

The Long Road to Hospital and Health Care Affiliation. Not every merger goes according to plan. For instance, our experience with RWDSU, the Retail, Wholesale, and Department Store Union, and its union within a union, the National Union of Hospital and Health Care Workers, better known as 1199, was a bumpy ride, to say the least. Leon Davis, 1199's president, seemed to be encouraging RWDSU to pursue a merger.

The discussion began early in 1979 while I was president of 32B-32J. Since RWDSU and 1199 were both headquartered in New York, it was natural for me to get talks started. I had worked with a lot of RWDSU people, such as Sam Kovenetsky, on local labor issues and political campaigns. I had known Jerry Brown, 1199's district officer in New England, since he was a kid because his father, Ken Brown, and I had worked together in politics. In fact, I was the one who steered Jerry to 1199 in the first place. I was a friend of Moe Foner, 1199's political strategist and public relations director, best known for the Bread and Roses cultural program that brought the arts to union members.

I also got along very well with Leon Davis. He used to enjoy educating me on his early days, telling me, "I was on one side of Seventh Avenue organizing the pharmacies, and on the other side were some of your top leaders, Dave Sullivan, Tom Shortman, Arthur Harckham, Tom Young, organizing the building service people. We'd be waving or hollering across the street to each other."

Official talks got underway in February 1979 between SEIU President George Hardy and RWDSU President Al Heaps. The hope was that 1199 and SEIU – two progressive unions – could work together to create a major opportunity for organizing health care workers. When I became president of SEIU in 1980 we continued to meet almost monthly. 1199 was all for moving forward with the merger, but RWDSU had concerns about their loss of autonomy and the issue of merging the two pension plans.

We eventually worked out our major differences and finalized an agreement with 1199. So when I addressed the national 1199 convention early in December 1981, I thought all systems were go. But right before I spoke, RWDSU's President Heaps walked off the stage in a huff. Internal problems and the politics that mergers inevitably involved had apparently changed Heaps' mind.

But the biggest obstacle to the merger had nothing to do with me, SEIU, or political rivalries: On December 30, 1981, a pipe bomb disguised as a Christmas package exploded in RWDSU headquarters, severely injuring Al Heaps. It was a shocking, dreadful, insane attack. When somebody in our office heard the news on the radio, I immediately went down to the hospital where Al had been taken. Al's wife and Lenore Miller, a vice president of RWDSU, were there. I did not see Al – he was in intensive care – so I sat outside the room and talked with Lenore. Primarily I was there to see what we could do to help the family. When I did see Al a few days later, there were no business discussions. It was a relatively long recovery period. The explosion left an impact on Al's life, his thinking.

I cannot say I know why, but Al Heaps announced the suspension of the merger from his hospital bed. That raised questions in some people's minds. But since the merger had been proceeding in a positive direction, there was no reason to think it was related to this attack. RWDSU, 1199, and SEIU were going through this process very thoughtfully, addressing structural concerns, the terms of employment of people in the unions, and who would continue to have a leadership role.

Then, as now, I really had no idea who could have done this. It could have been some disgruntled person, it could have been something to do with outsiders. Certainly some local unions and some leaders opposed the merger, but I did not see any indication that people were of a mind to resort to violence. The fact that they never uncovered where the bomb came from just shows how difficult it is to find the real culprits in a situation like this. But it sure scared the hell out of a lot of people.

Later, much later, a merger of sorts did occur, just not the one we were planning. In 1984 the National Union of Hospital and Health Care Workers left RWDSU, and in 1989 a majority of 1199 locals joined SEIU. The whole enterprise was more complicated than this sounds, as part of 1199 had negotiated an agreement join AFSCME. So there were Article XX charges filed before a settlement vote was negotiated. Ultimately, it all worked out.

One Million Members Strong. By 1991, SEIU had hit the one-million member mark and became the fastest growing AFL-CIO affiliate. So we knew we were on the right track as far as diversifying and strengthening our membership. But while our campaign to attract public employee and health care affiliates was proving very effective, we were not doing so well with our original core membership group – the janitors, elevator operators, doormen, and other building service workers who gave me my start in the union. We had maintained union density in New York City where we built the powerhouse local union, 32BJ. Its members were still the highest paid building service workers in the country, and they enjoyed good benefit programs. Local 1 in Chicago, the Flat Janitors' Union, was also still fairly strong. Unfortunately, many of the original local janitors' unions were in disrepair, and employers were taking advantage of that. We knew we needed to rebuild the janitors' base or risk losing our hold in that sector.

Contributing to our problem was the changing nature of the building service industry. When I was coming up, building owners generally employed their own janitorial staffs, so we were able to build strong relationships over time. But now owners were contracting work out to cleaning companies, and they rewarded the lowest bidder. To keep from losing their contracts, the cleaning companies kept wages low and benefits were out of the question.

"Justice for Janitors" Is Born in Pittsburgh. That is how it looked in 1985 when the Office Building Association of Pittsburgh locked out 450 members of Local 29. The contractors and the local building owners were going for broke: they were looking to cut wages at least 15 percent. But the members were not about to give in. They managed to attract attention to their problem right away. They organized a bus trip to Columbus, Ohio, where they picketed the corporate headquarters of a major real estate developer – and not just any developer. It was John W. Galbreath, who had just sold his interest in the Pittsburgh Pirates.

Pittsburgh is known as the City of Churches, and that was a good thing for us. A number of Catholic priests supported the janitors from the start, including Monsignor Charles Owen Rice. He was an outspoken individual with a national reputation who had been working with unions since he started out as a parish priest in the 1930s. Monsignor Rice kept the janitors' story alive by writing newspaper articles, giving radio interviews, and doing whatever he could to support the strikers. Pretty soon the entire community was standing with the janitors and against the big property owners.

One cleaning company, the National Cleaning Contractors, settled with the union before any of the others did. National serviced two buildings owned by Mellon Bank, a prominent Pittsburgh institution.

But even before the ink on that union contract was dry, Mellon fired National and hired a new nonunion contractor who drastically cut wages and hours. What was once a full-time, 40-hour-a-week job that paid around $240 was now an eight-hour-a-week part-time job that paid around $32. That was certainly not a family wage, unless every member of the family, including the kids, worked two jobs. As far as Mellon was concerned, the wages and hours of the contractor's employees were none of their business.

But SEIU decided to make it Mellon's business. We had hired some pretty aggressive organizers, and they brought in creative ideas to mobilize workers and generate public support. We also hired some very talented researchers who knew how to find out what was really going on with company labor practices. Up against a business community led by the wealthy and powerful Mellon Bank, we were ready to take our case to the public.

We parked ourselves outside Mellon bank branches and distributed around 20,000 leaflets that zeroed in on the bank's values. We asked questions like: "Why are Mellon's high-paid corporate managers working so hard to break the backs of hard-working janitors?" We filed unfair labor practice charges. We filed suits. We held a major rally at Mellon Square in the heart of Pittsburgh's central business district. The SEIU really pushed this campaign. The workers themselves came up with the slogan that captured the spirit behind the campaign. On their homemade signs, the words "Justice for Janitors" said it all.

We certainly got attention that summer, as my friend, the late Bill Wynn, former president of the United Food and Commercial Workers, liked to remind me. He played golf in those days in Florida with a group of retirees. One day as they ate lunch together after their round of golf, there on the TV was film of me, outside the Mellon Bank, demonstrating with the janitors in Pittsburgh. One of the golfers said, "Oh, shut that bastard off. He's going to have us all organized if we don't get rid of him."

"Well, he's a friend of mine," Bill told him.

"What? What did you do before you retired?"

"I was president of the United Food and Commercial Workers." Well, that was the end of the conversation – and the last time Bill played golf with that crowd.

Rethinking Our Organizing Strategies. There were always those who said low-wage workers like janitors could not be organized, or organized for long. But I was not one of them. My experiences with Local 32BJ taught me that aggressive organizing, political action, strategic economic leverage, and a militant strike now and then can move employers to unionize.

But the shift to contract cleaning by the mid-1980s, coupled with an economic recession, growing anti-union sentiments around the country, and a new immigrant workforce, required a change in our thinking. Now the questions were: How do we move workers to organize given the risks they face?

How do you engage newly arrived immigrant men and women, who rarely speak English and often lack documentation? And how do you persuade existing locals to organize new work, not just protect the work they have?

Especially after our experience in Pittsburgh, I had faith that we could find new answers – and I was smart enough to surround myself with a talented staff who not only shared my belief that it could be done, but were determined to make it happen. Stephen Lerner, who was hired around this time to direct our building service organizing campaign, certainly brought a new, critical eye and a creative enthusiasm to the project. The workers in Pittsburgh coined the phrase "Justice for Janitors," but with Stephen's help it became a national organizing campaign.

Pittsburgh taught us to pressure building owners, not contractors, a lesson we took to Denver, the first stop on our new campaign. Denver presented a new situation – the so-called "double-breasted" contractors who worked under union contracts at the airport, for instance, but worked non-union in the private sector. We started with a top-down strategy: Instead of striking those contractors, Local 105 put pressure on those who hired them – the political appointees on the airport's governing boards – to fire double-breasted contractors unless they agreed to recognize the union on all their jobs.

We also learned to work from the bottom up. Traditionally we had organized janitors by going building-to-building to sign up workers, petition for a union election, and negotiate the contract. But Denver's unorganized janitors reminded us that the building-by-building method of organizing was not going to work. Their building owners had told them that they would just replace their contractor with a cheaper one if they pushed for a union contract. Under those conditions, these workers had no interest in unionizing building-by-building. They were, however, extremely interested in Stephen's idea to organize the whole city at once.

So these nonunion workers were not anti-union – they were anti-unemployment. And these new immigrants were not un-organizable, either. Once they were on board with our citywide strategy, they proved time and time again that they were willing to take risks. They just needed a realistic chance of winning.

The Top-Down, Bottom-Up Corporate Campaign. Denver became a model top-down, bottom-up corporate campaign. We worked with janitors across the city; we analyzed how contractors competed with each other and how they marketed their services; and we put pressure on building owners by disturbing their peace. Our loud demonstrations were legendary. Then we used whatever leverage we had to let the public know how the rich building owners were mistreating their poor service workers: We filed charges with the Department of Labor when workers were underpaid or misclassified as "independent contractors" to deprive them of benefits and protections; we notified OSHA, the Occupational Safety and Health Administration, when conditions were unsafe; and we publicized our discoveries through leaflets, rallies, newspaper articles, advertisements, and whatever other outlets we had. Ultimately our goal was to persuade building owners that signing with the union was a good business decision.

One of my favorite tactics even got Santa Claus working for us. At a downtown Denver bank we were picketing, we had Santa Claus distributing leaflets. When Santa entered the bank and refused to leave, he was promptly arrested. The picture of police escorting him out was widely featured in the news, giving us valuable publicity.

Justice for Janitors organizing tactics were aggressive, but for good reasons. First, we wanted to grab the public's attention and get them to see these workers as real people with real needs who worked hard every day. We were hoping to turn the tide, as the organizers would say, by asking why, in the richest country in the world, did people who performed nasty but vital work, like cleaning toilets, fail to earn enough to feed their families. And second, we wanted the janitors to see for themselves that, collectively, they had the power to make a difference and to get people to listen to and respond to their story.

Taking Justice for Janitors on the Road. We won our organizing campaign in Pittsburgh and we won in Denver – and then we took Justice for Janitors on the road to Atlanta, to Los Angeles, to Washington, D.C., and some smaller cities, too. Wherever we went, we unleashed creative public protests and a barrage of lawsuits and wage-and-hour complaints. And our tactics brought results: By 1994 SEIU represented 20 percent of the building service workforce. One nonunion contractor gave this explanation for why he finally signed with the union: "There was no way of making them go away."

Justice for Janitors was exhilarating, it was creative, it was provocative and unconventional, but it was not easy. In Los Angeles, for instance, our effort to organize Century City janitors ended in violence. The Los Angeles Police Department used batons to beat 450 workers who were marching towards a Century City park for a demonstration. Several people were seriously injured and one poor pregnant woman on the march actually suffered a miscarriage. The beatings were captured on film, and while no one wanted things to end this way, those brutal images marked a turning point in that campaign. It was not too long before the Mexican and Central American immigrants who kept Century City's buildings clean had the benefits of a union contract.

Blocking the Bridge. Washington, D.C., was another tough battle. It may be the capital of the United States, but D.C. is basically a Southern town – meaning it's a nonunion town and the building owners there intended to keep it that way. They say imitation is the best form of flattery, so I suppose SEIU should have been flattered that the Apartment and Office Building Association took a page from the Justice for Janitors book. The owners' association members set up a legal defense fund, hired a notorious anti-union lawyer, and waged their own legal and public relations campaign against us.

D.C. was one of the toughest cities we faced. But the organizers did a tremendous job of breaking down barriers between the old union membership, which was largely African American, and the new Latino work force. They used a lot of dramatic tactics that played on the "Tale of Two Cities" theme: one D.C. made up of rich, white movers and shakers in commercial real estate, and another D.C. of poor black and brown workers with minimum-wage jobs and no benefits. The Washington demonstrators set up a shantytown called "Janitorville" right by the World Bank, where some of the most exploited janitors were employed. Singer Harry Belafonte, who was performing at the Kennedy Center, came down to support them, as he had once been a janitor himself. He even autographed one of the brochures they were handing out that read, "What does the World Bank do? Keep black people broke."

A couple of ads ran in the *Washington Post*, pointing out that some of the biggest, richest building owners, like Oliver Carr, did not pay their fair share of taxes. This was when D.C. was in bad financial straits and was under the thumb of a Financial Control Board, whose chairman was a director at Carr Realty. The control board was cutting school funds, public safety funds, and other things that really mattered to working-class people.

Our D.C. tactics culminated in the demonstrations that became the emblem of the Justice for Janitors campaign. In December 1994, 200 members of D.C.'s Local 82 shut down the 14th Street Bridge for 45 minutes during rush hour. They used a car to block this major commuter route from the Virginia suburbs, and they hung up banners with the message, "D.C. has Carr trouble." Four months later, they did it again.

Oliver Carr's people said we were a publicity-seeking nuisance. And we *were* a nuisance. Even my good friend Steve Coyle, of the AFL-CIO Housing Investment Trust, who got caught in the back-up, begged me to give him a heads up the next time we planned to block the bridge. Another good friend, Senator Ted Kennedy, let me know that he was none too pleased when the campaign made him late for a committee meeting on Capitol Hill. Plenty of area residents did not see the connection between Oliver Carr, our blocking the bridge, and gaining justice for janitors. But as one of our organizers told the *Washington Post*, the janitors waged this political fight to advance their economic interests. Blocking the bridge was a surefire way to get their side of the story out.

Lessons from the Janitors Campaign. Justice for Janitors was a commitment we made to organize the unorganized janitors, and we really were fortunate to have great people on our staff who were interested in doing this. The campaign had a tremendous impact on our grassroots activities and it made a tremendous impression on other union leaders and on rank-and-file workers all over the country. As I traveled from one city to the next, people would ask me about the campaign because they had seen stories in the news. When you can get so many different people from so many different places to respond to your story, I think that is the mark of a successful publicity campaign. And I know we did that because to this day people still ask me, "Have you blocked any bridges recently?"

The fact that we were able to cause such a stir and still generate support for the janitors convinced me that SEIU was on the right track. And it got me wondering whether Justice for Janitors could be an organizing model for the future – not just for building service workers, but for the labor movement as a whole.

4

NEW VOICES: CAMPAIGNING
FOR AFL-CIO REFORMS

With the country's workforce becoming more diverse, I felt that SEIU was the face of the future of organized labor – and I worked hard to move the union in that direction. Long before "diversity" became a national buzzword, SEIU was diverse. We had male and female members and leaders, black, brown, and white, going back to the union's very beginning. We had building service workers, public employees, health care workers, clericals, and even some retail workers. We had Irish, Italian, Jamaican, Puerto Rican, Chinese, and so many others including a new generation of Central American immigrants. Our members were old and young, gay and straight, socially conservative and as liberal as you could get. Some were bona fide radicals.

SEIU was also a very democratic union, with a culture more open to voicing new ideas and criticism than what I have seen in other labor unions. We had a reputation for getting into controversial issues, like abortion rights or U.S. foreign policy. We also spent a lot of time debating how we operated as a union and whether the international union was truly responsive to the local unions' needs in terms of finances, programs, or assistance. These could be very complex discussions. SEIU had a reputation for making sure that we were touching base with our local unions on these issues and making sure that everyone got their say. This participatory style of leadership was quite a contrast to the many more traditional trade unions.

Consensus-Based Leadership at SEIU. I used to joke that I was the most progressive member of Local 32B, but as SEIU president, I found myself out front on some issues, and more in the middle on others. But my opinion was just that – my opinion. As SEIU president I had to be respectful of all positions on a particular issue, and I sometimes had to go easy on my own personal preferences. I think that I was fairly able to balance those kinds of discussions and to recognize the positions of different people and encourage them to talk to each other. That was the key: Talking these various issues out. So as a union, we did not rush to force issues. We developed a process that allowed time for discussion.

At each convention, we were constantly seeking to improve the opportunities to hear from members on issues that mattered to them. For instance, when we were developing our convention agendas, we would get as much grassroots involvement as possible through our regular regional meetings. The real challenge was making sure the organization had a process in place to address controversial issues at the right time, either prior to a convention or in the convention itself.

Our concern with building consensus from the bottom up, not the top down, grew out of our experience with affiliating independent associations like CSEA. We saw the advantage of opening up discussions on gay rights, for example, not only because it was the right thing to do, but also because it opened our doors to folks who might not otherwise have been inclined to affiliate with us. When independent associations saw how we operated, they realized how becoming part of a bigger entity would make their voices that much stronger.

Taking a Stand on Gay Rights. When it came to gay rights and support for organizations like Pride at Work, we were among the frontrunners. For the most part, that was stimulated by organizers, leaders, and convention delegates who had a lot of personal experience and took a very strong position on this issue.

Through these discussions, I got a first-class education in the high personal and professional costs of hostility in the workplace. It made a real impact on me. At the 1983 AFL-CIO convention, I urged delegates to adopt a resolution to prohibit discrimination based on sexual orientation in housing, employment, public accommodations, credit, and government service. "We in the labor movement don't believe that civil rights are a special interest," I said. "It's all our interest. It's the interest of us all to ensure that equality and freedom are extended to all the citizens of our country." As I looked around the room, I could sense the hesitation. But I am pleased to say the AFL-CIO adopted the resolution and not one delegate spoke out against it. At SEIU's convention the following year, we passed a similar resolution and added sexual orientation to our definition of diversity. As the AIDS crisis mounted, we also pushed to increase federal funding for AIDS research.

Questioning AFL-CIO's Foreign Policy Positions. U.S. policy in Central America, long supported by the AFL-CIO, was another vigorously debated issue at SEIU's 1984 convention. A strong contingent of delegates definitely expected SEIU to take a leadership role in shifting American foreign policy. Whether it was because SEIU had a growing contingent of members from Central America, or whether it reflected the membership's overall concern with social justice issues and belief that the CIA was trampling on the democratic rights of people in Guatemala, El Salvador, and Nicaragua, we wanted to do whatever was right for these people.

As with the other major issues, we had strong differences of opinion in our ranks. But our goal was to analyze the situation and its component parts. At the time, many SEIU members questioned the AFL-CIO's strong anti-communist stand – some even referred to it as the AFL-CIA. And that became important in terms of how they related to the AFL-CIO and its president, Lane Kirkland. [2]

The AFL-CIO foreign policy positions, with which many at SEIU took issue, had grown out of a strong post-World War II agenda of free trade unionism that was based on anti-communism abroad and full employment at home. For many years, first under the AFL-CIO's founding president George Meany and then under Kirkland, the AFL-CIO's international policy opposed the Soviet Union, supported U.S. defense spending, and expected government support for labor's international efforts to promote democratic trade unions abroad. [3]

As SEIU began to debate our policy stance in Central America, we questioned the AFL-CIO's support of U.S. policy there. A couple of our local leaders used their vacations to travel to these countries and meet with union representatives, some who supported their governments, and some who did not. The goal was to find out what the Central American people wanted us to do, and it appeared they wanted a negotiated peace settlement rather than a U.S.-backed regional war. When our visiting leaders asked what we could do to help the situation, they heard the same reply, over and over: End the U.S. military aid to Central America and work to defeat Ronald Reagan's reelection.

Based on these on-the-ground discussions, we hammered out a position that we presented at our 1984 SEIU convention. We adopted a compromise that made clear not only our opposition to U.S. intervention in Central America but also our intention to let the AFL-CIO know where we stood. So we used our resolution to encourage the AFL-CIO to do as we had been doing internally in opening up the discussion and the debate. We wanted the leadership to take a hard look at their position on Central

America and to bring in experts from both sides of the aisle who had different positions.

By opening up the process at SEIU, we were able to have a full discussion about these international issues. But it was tough trying to educate folks to take an objective look at all this. We managed to avoid a floor fight at our 1984 convention, but that was not the end of the discussion. Our Committee on International Affairs, led by Marc Earls, the president of Local 6 in Seattle and an international vice president, was probably our busiest committee at our next few conventions.

And that led to another serious discussion, one that was focused on how the AFL-CIO operated and whether the leadership was listening to membership and moving in the right direction. But more about that later.

President Reagan Fires the Air Traffic Controllers. When Lane Kirkland took over as president of the AFL-CIO in 1979, it was a pretty critical time in AFL-CIO history. The following year, Ronald Reagan was elected president and our influence had started to slide. Reagan's victory in 1980 signaled the start of a bad deal for America's workers. It was a bitter lesson for those in labor's ranks who had thought their interests could possibly be served by this former president of the Screen Actors Guild.

When President Reagan broke the Air Traffic Controllers' strike in the summer of 1981, he gave the 13,000 PATCO members an ultimatum: return to work in 48 hours or lose their jobs. And over 11,000 PATCO members lost their jobs when they continued to strike despite a ban on work stoppages by government unions. Worse, the fired workers were no longer eligible for any kind of federal employment. The Professional Air Traffic Controllers Organization – which ironically had been one of only three unions to support Reagan's election – lost its certification to represent workers later that year.

Within a few days of the PATCO firings, Lane Kirkland was invited to the White House. He asked about a dozen of us to come with him. After we had waited 10 or 15 minutes, President Reagan came in. He had about six people with him: Secretary of Labor Ray Donovan; Vice President George H.W. Bush; Elizabeth Dole, who was on the White House staff at the time; and a few others. He opened up by saying he knew why we were there, it was a very unfortunate situation, but he had to obey the law and had to take the actions that he took, and it was very hard for him to do.

When the president finished, he called on Lane, and Lane gave the remarks that you would expect him to give about what a serious situation this was and how these workers did not deserve that kind of punishment, and the impact that it had on their lives and their families.

Then the president called on J.J. O'Donnell, who was the president of the Air Line Pilots Association. J.J. was a Republican and had supported Reagan for president. Fortunately, his labor union background came through. He pointed out how important an issue this was to the pilots, because of potential safety issues, that the air traffic controllers did not deserve this, and he pleaded for the president to change things.

And then Al Shanker, president of the American Federation of Teachers, raised his hand. Al was no stranger to public employee strikes and had spent time in jail after taking New York City teachers on strike. When the president saw Al Shanker's hand go up, he knew he was in for some words that he would not like to hear. Just then a Secret Service person came up and placed an index card against the president's coffee cup. "Oh, my God, is it that time already? It feels like we just got started. I'm sorry, I have this Brezhnev call that I've been expecting. George, you're going to have to take over and I'm going to have to excuse myself." And out he went, and from there the meeting just went downhill.

Rising Anti-Union Sentiment. There is no question that Ronald Reagan's attack on the Air Traffic Controllers was a serious blow, not only to the controllers but to millions more working men and women, particularly those who were union members. The president's hard line stance radically altered industrial and political relations with unions and emboldened the right wing to promote anti-union laws and actions. Once Reagan made it acceptable to hire replacement workers, employers followed his example with a vengeance. The White House had declared open season on workers and their families. Reagan's absolute lack of compassion for these individuals was shocking. Yes, the decision of these public employees to strike was dangerous and controversial; but the punishment – that these strikers could never return to their jobs – was excessive. Some strikers lost their homes to foreclosure; some committed suicide. It seemed to me that if the president had an ounce of decency, he would have tried to deal with the human costs of his decision.

Leading the huge Solidarity Day march in Washington, with SEIU secretary-treasurer Richard Cordtz and my young daughter Trish, to protest the Reagan Administration's labor policies after the firing of the Air Traffic Controllers.

Lane certainly tried. He had already gotten the AFL-CIO Executive Council to approve plans for a march to protest the president's social and economic policies and the program cuts that went along with them, so the timing was right. A few weeks later in September, half a million union members marched in Washington, D.C., to protest Reaganomics and defend the PATCO strikers. This Solidarity Day March was the largest U.S. labor march in history. At the time, though, no one was ready to block any bridges.

AFL-CIO's Political Response. With Ronald Reagan dead set against us, the AFL-CIO decided to play a bigger role in politics: In the early 1980s, the Federation became the Democratic Party's most reliable – and generous – contributor. Our contributions went a long way to funding the Democratic National Committee, and Democratic congressional candidates facing tough campaigns knew they could count on us for help. But as it turned out, we did not get much in return. Democrat or Republican, Congress ignored our calls for health care reform, legislation to ban striker replacements, an increase in the minimum wage, and all the rest of our legislative agenda.

So by 1983 Lane Kirkland decided to help a pro-labor Democrat become president, and for the first time in our history, the AFL-CIO endorsed a primary candidate – Walter "Fritz" Mondale, the long-time liberal Minnesota senator and Jimmy Carter's vice president. But that did not work out as Lane planned. Mondale won the nomination, but Republicans claimed that labor's endorsement proved he was the captive of special interests. When the votes were counted, Reagan won with more than half of all union voters on his side. And that was after we contributed around $35 million to Mondale's campaign. So there was a definite gap between the leadership's and the membership's political point of view.

I had worked hard in that campaign, and Mondale's loss was a big disappointment. Could we have done more? Of course. We certainly could have mobilized more at the grassroots level, a strategy that had been very successful for SEIU.

At SEIU we had a lot of success getting our members to the polls in 1984 because we actively educated them on how elections affect them and their families. We focused on legislative issues that were important to them and to their lives, whether it was in terms of strengthening the union or providing better safety on the job. We tried to give them more education on the importance of politics and legislation so they could draw the parallel between their job and their vote. We helped them see how increasing the minimum wage benefited them and how changes to any labor law might have an impact on their lives. Safety and health, as an example, became a big issue for health care workers. Tax issues and budget cuts were particularly important to public workers. It was not that our members didn't already know some of this, but they had not paid it that much attention. In addition to the presidential election, we stressed that it mattered to us, as union members, who we had representing us in the state capital, or in city hall, or in Congress.

So we would bring rank-and-file leaders together to coordinate their plans. It was like an organizing campaign, a political organizing campaign. We would give them some goals to achieve and impress upon them how valuable their activity was. Anytime I spoke to them I would say, "I can go speak to any number of members of Congress, but it's your personal contact, your one-on-one discussion with your member of Congress that is important to him." I think they had to hear it to realize the value of their work and to spur them on to do more.

A Few Big Political Successes. Bright political moments were few and far between in the 1980s and early '90s. Perhaps our biggest success came in

1990 when the labor movement helped elect Minnesota's Paul Wellstone to the Senate. What a wonderful human being he was. He was the closest we had to another Hubert Humphrey, the long-time Minnesota senator who fought so hard for working people. Paul articulated our issues so well. He supported our position on trade and on raising the minimum wage, and he advocated a national health care system and labor law reform. I always enjoyed when he would say, "I represent the Democratic wing of the Democratic Party." It was a real tragedy for everyone – his family, the labor movement, our country – when Paul and his lovely wife and daughter were killed in a plane crash as he was seeking a third term in the Senate.

We also had a few bright policy moments too. With the merger of SEIU and the 1199 locals, SEIU became the nation's largest health care workers union and a leader in health care policy, especially at the federal level. Mary Kay Henry, for instance, who joined SEIU as a researcher in 1981 and became SEIU President in 2010, played a leading role. She became the head of the union's health care division and led the early field campaign calling for health care reform. In the late 1980s, rapidly increasing health care costs spurred interest in health care reform among unions, health care advocates, and even businesses. Then in 1991, Harris Wofford's incredibly successful campaign running for U.S. Senate in a special election brought the issue of health care reform to national attention. SEIU, with Mary Kay's help on the ground, started a campaign that propelled it to the center of national conversation during a presidential election year.

Bill Clinton's election as president in 1992 was probably the next brightest moment. I got to know him early on in the campaign. He was interested in an AFL-CIO endorsement, but before that could happen we had to get to know him, his personality, his values, and everything else. We reached out to each other and had phone conversations, and it was a very easy kind of discussion. In my humble opinion, he was saying the right things, for the most part, as far as the labor movement was concerned. He also impressed me as a person who could actually get elected.

In our private conversations, I expressed some unions' concerns about his position on trade policy. We were not seeking an apology for his past positions; we were looking for him to take a hard look at his position on trade, and he did that. Clinton also took my suggestion to reach out to the affiliates who had strong concerns about this, like the United Auto Workers and the Steelworkers. I think that he was very convincing, and that is his nature.

Another problem was Clinton's track record with the Arkansas labor movement as governor of that state. At the AFL-CIO meeting to discuss an endorsement, the president of the Arkansas labor movement, Bill Becker, was in the audience. So Clinton recognized him in his remarks with a comment like, "We haven't always agreed, but I understand that Bill was representing workers, and I admire him for that."

We were also considering Tom Harkin, the Iowa senator who was especially well known for his positions on the industrial unions' issues. All of us in the labor movement had great respect for Tom.

But when it came to the AFL-CIO's endorsement, we thought that Clinton could win not only the nomination, but the election. I was a principal player at that meeting and one of Clinton's strongest supporters. Although there were those who still had reservations, I believe that we made the right choice.

Mixed Record of the Bill Clinton Years. As president, Bill Clinton certainly had a good relationship with the labor movement and was accessible. He made some very good appointments, too. Overall, I think that he really did strive to improve the lives of working people through his programs and his policies. Could he have been stronger? Probably so. His nature, which you cannot criticize, is to really try and bring people together – to try and bring labor and management together. While I think labor proved how interested we were in trying to do that, we were never able to really get significant support from the other side. In the health care debate, for example, we had some major employers supporting Hillary Clinton's plan. But without the Business Roundtable or the Chamber of Commerce on board, those backers did not matter.

The president's support for NAFTA – the North American Free Trade Agreement – was another disappointment. I remember when President George H.W. Bush was pushing hard for NAFTA, he said trade meant jobs and more trade meant higher incomes for American workers. Then Bill Clinton picked up the refrain. Talk about false promises. Lane Kirkland called it an atrocity that served one interest only: the moneyed interest.

In our fight against NAFTA, we were basically asking for two things: tough workers' rights language, and environmental protections. We did not get either one, even after Lane threatened to withhold AFL-CIO support from any Democrat who voted for NAFTA (an empty threat, as it turned out). It did not help that our friend Clinton accused us of using "rough-shod, muscle-bound tactics" to try and defeat NAFTA. He might as well have called us "goons."

The AFL-CIO was deeply disappointed in the mid-term elections of 1994 when Republicans gained control of both the House and the Senate for the first time in 40 years. Now we had to deal with a speaker of the House, Newt Gingrich, who never missed a chance to put down "big labor bosses"; a new Senate majority leader, Dick Armey, who thought that minimum wage laws were "bad public policy"; and the labor haters, race baiters, and women and children bashers elected along with them. So that mid-term defeat turned out to be a real wake-up call.

Questioning the AFL-CIO Leadership. The steady defeats of the early '90s – on NAFTA, labor law reform, health care reform, and the 1994 mid-term elections – got us thinking hard about where the labor movement was headed. Some of the AFL-CIO's largest affiliates, including SEIU, AFSCME, and the United Auto Workers, among others, began to debate whether the AFL-CIO should concentrate on lobbying elected officials for change, or whether it should develop and fund more grassroots political education and mobilization campaigns. We also wondered whether the AFL-CIO leadership was doing enough to broaden the movement and promote a positive image for labor. Ever since Ronald Reagan made hiring replacement workers acceptable, our opponents had been calling the AFL-CIO a "paper tiger," threatening but ineffectual.

All this raised the uncomfortable question: Was Lane Kirkland still the right man for the job?

To be fair, Lane was trying, at least to some extent. In fact, when he took over from George Meany, he was considered a reformer: Lane negotiated agreements to bring the Teamsters, the United Auto Workers, and the United Mine Workers, among others, back into the AFL-CIO. He brought together labor unions, civil rights activists, feminists, and other liberal groups when he organized the successful 1981 Solidarity Day March and the Solidarity Days that followed over the next few years. And that had not happened in a very long time.

He also appointed the first woman, Joyce Miller of the Alalgamated Clothing Workers of America, to the AFL-CIO Executive Council, a big step and one that was long overdue, considering the large number of women union members. And it was on his watch that the AFL-CIO established the Organizing Institute, to train new recruits and develop new strategies, and the Labor Institute of Public Affairs, which launched the "Union Yes" public relations campaign. Even though he did not like appearing on television himself, Lane recognized that the Federation had to be more active and use mass media to promote itself.

But there was a growing feeling among the affiliates that he had not gone far enough; he had not produced enough change to satisfy a majority of the AFL-CIO. Whether it was his fault or not, the fact remained that labor's share of the workforce dropped from 23 percent in 1979 when Lane came to office to around 15 percent in 1994, and our bargaining power, political clout, and media visibility dropped along with it. At the same time, a lot of the membership questioned the Federation's international policy – a left-right split had already developed over issues like the war in El Salvador. So more and more I was hearing from individual leaders of a growing interest in seeing some real change. Instead of a Washington-based policy-making institution, they wanted the AFL-CIO to become a grassroots organizing, bargaining, and political machine that could speak up for, and stand up for, working families. Instead of wielding less and less power, they wanted to build up labor's power again.

A Call from Jerry McEntee. It was around June 1994 when AFSCME President Gerald "Jerry" McEntee called me and said, "John, we've got to talk about the AFLCIO." And talk we did – five, ten times over the next few months. We were unlikely allies, two presidents of unions that had long been at war in the public sector workplaces of America. But we agreed that we had no time to waste. We were not talking about who should be president of the AFL-CIO – that was not an issue yet. We were talking about where the AFLCIO was headed and what we could do about it. We felt we were being battered around and we did not have any response, no spokesperson.

So we came up with a plan we called "Project '95," a coordinated grassroots political action plan to mobilize the Federation's 13 million members and target the Republicans' most vulnerable candidates. When Lane was not interested in this idea, we were disappointed, to say the least. That is when Jerry started talking about a leadership change.

One thing to know about Jerry is that once he came to a belief about something, he would fight for it. And that turned out to be a real asset during, and beyond, this fight. Jerry saw the momentum building and he did not hesitate to speak out loud and clear. Lane and Tom Donahue, the AFL-CIO's secretary-treasurer, held an annual series of regional meetings that brought together local unions, state federations, central labor councils, and so on. Jerry not only started going to these regional meetings but raising issues about change.

Jerry was also encouraging individual union presidents to talk together about how we would pursue this. We never met as a group; it was just a series of oneonone discussions with other union leaders. But soon it became clear that there was a core group of union leaders representing a majority of AFLCIO members who were unhappy with the AFL-CIO's direction. I do not think any of us wanted to see Lane hurt, but we were hopeful that he would be convinced that it was time for a change.

Conversation with Lane Kirkland. After talking to Jerry, I decided that I should have a conversation with Lane. We met that summer and I explained to him that members of the Executive Council were interested in change. He knew that; he had supporters who had let him know what was going on. I told him that people wondered whether he was planning to retire, or whether he had considered taking on a new area of work, or even part-time involvement. Some thought that he might be interested in being the ambassador to Poland. Right away he said, "I've already turned that down." I said, "I don't think any of our folks know that," but maybe some of them did.

Then I mentioned that a lot of people thought that he would support Tom Donahue for election as president the following year at the 1995 AFL-CIO convention. Lane did not pick up on that, which was surprising and disappointing because we knew how hard Tom had worked. Whether Tom would have changed things as much as they needed to be changed, had he been elected, I do not know. But in any event, Lane did not comment or express any support for Tom.

He did want to know who was speaking out against him, so I mentioned George Kourpias, president of the Machinists. George had agreed that I could raise his name. Then Lane went over to his desk and put in a call to George, and George confirmed it. George told Lane that he was hearing a lot of concerns from his members and their leaders. George also mentioned that his union's practice is for the president to retire at the age of 65. Lane was 72 at the time.

I did not hear Lane make any comments. He got off the phone and he did not repeat the conversation to me, but it was clear that he was upset with what he had heard. I believe that that was the end of our conversation. We parted in a respectful way.

Our Concerns Go Public. Our campaign for change at the AFL-CIO went public in January 1995 when the *Washington Post* reported that "unnamed labor leaders" acknowledged their dissatisfaction with Lane Kirkland. Jerry McEntee later admitted that he had contributed to the story. By that time I felt pretty strongly that it was time for new leadership. I had worked very closely with Lane and with Tom, but I was convinced that we had exhausted all of the other options.

I met with Lane again in February 1995 to talk about putting more resources into organizing, and the need for a transition and change in leadership, but he still was not interested. He did not want to talk about retiring or having Tom Donahue succeed him.

So when I went down to Florida a short time later for an AFL-CIO Executive Council meeting, the move towards an election campaign was getting underway. A group of us got together at the Fontainebleau Hotel, where AFSCME's leaders were meeting – a little removed from where the

AFL-CIO council meeting was going on – to see if our supporters could convince additional union presidents to participate.

We made our plans, and when the council went into executive session, we let Lane know what was on our minds. The discussion, chaired by Lane, started off when he acknowledged that some of us were dissatisfied. "So what's the beef?" he asked.

Then he went around the table. Individuals expressed themselves, some in support of his presidency, and some expressing dissatisfaction. Lane took the critical comments in a personal way. Jerry was very hard on Lane throughout the whole campaign, and this meeting was no exception. But while he did not mince words, Jerry was not aiming at Lane personally. He was saying what he thought needed to be said to move us forward. It took a lot of courage and confidence to do that, traits that ran strong in Jerry's character. But that kind of criticism can be hard for a person to accept, especially at that stage of his life when he might expect recognition for the indisputably good contributions he had made.

When it was my turn, I acknowledged all those good things, but I also said, "There are many of us who feel it's time for a change." I tried to be as respectful as I could, but I had made up my mind. And so had a lot of other folks, who now believed we were doing the right thing.

By Any Means Necessary. I was not looking to leave SEIU. I was very happy with what I was able to do with the strong political support I had internally, and I really liked the work I was doing. So I was not thinking of higher office when I sent around a memo to the affiliates questioning the AFL-CIO's current leadership and stating that the "decline of the labor movement must be stopped by any means necessary."

I was still taking the position that I expected Tom Donahue would succeed Lane in October if Lane did not run for reelection, and in my memo I endorsed Tom for president. But Tom, I think, felt there was little chance that Lane would retire at that time, so in May 1995 he announced his own retirement. He said he was stepping down at the end of his term in October to end any speculation that he might be a candidate for the AFLCIO presidency. In the letter he sent around to Executive Council members, he said that he had been part of Lane's administration for 16 years and supported every policy that the AFL-CIO followed during those years. Right after that, Lane held a press conference to say, "If nominated I will stand. If elected I will serve."

With Lane seeking reelection and Tom out of the running, Jerry McEntee announced that AFSCME and 10 other unions, including SEIU – what we called the Group of Eleven – would not be endorsing Lane and were putting together a slate of candidates to run against him as national officers. This was a very big deal. Never since Samuel Gompers founded the American Federation of Labor in 1896 had anyone challenged an election at that level. Jerry put it this way: "We're singing from a new songbook. This has never been done before."

We had the Steelworkers, the Auto Workers, the Laborers, the Operating Engineers, the Paper Workers, the Teamsters, the Machinists, the Carpenters, and the Mine Workers on our side, along with AFSCME and SEIU. But Lane had a lot of support, too. The United Food and Commercial Workers stayed with Lane. And so did Bob Georgine, the president of the Building and Construction Trades Department, and the majority of the building trades unions.

A lot of Lane Kirkland's support was personal. People did not want him to be embarrassed by having it appear that he was being pushed out. Others felt strongly about avoiding a public fight. Al Shanker and others who valued Lane's international policies thought that the opposition was a little too left and isolationist for the AFL-CIO's good. At the time, Tom Donahue was urging me and the others to support Lane. He thought that

Lane could be convinced to serve less than a full term. But we were determined to press on.

I believed strongly that the American labor movement had become irrelevant to the vast majority of unorganized workers, and maybe to organized workers, too. With the Cold War now over, the AFL-CIO should spend less on foreign operations, and more on organizing, particularly on multiunion, industrywide campaigns. I called for more grassroots political organizing and for conditioning our support of political candidates on their support of labor issues in return.

And finally, I wanted the AFL-CIO to give a greater voice and more power to female and minority workers who were a vital part of our membership. While the new workforce was increasingly younger, and filled with more people of color, an older generation of white male leaders still dominated the Executive Council.

We were not battling over offices and personalities. We were battling over the future of the labor movement.

The Leadership Contest Takes Shape. In June 1995, probably because he realized the opposition had the votes to defeat him, Lane Kirkland decided to step down as president of the AFL-CIO. Tom Donahue changed his mind about retiring – in fact he was contacting union leaders to get their support for his presidency. He explained it this way: "I said that I would never be a candidate against Lane Kirkland, and since Lane has now indicated that he does not intend to run again, I have said that in light of that, I want to examine a candidacy which I believe can be a unity candidacy." Some people thought that because of our long friendship and mutual respect, I might help Tom forge a unity slate. But that opportunity was long gone. Frankly, at this point we thought Tom was too identified with Lane to be a real agent for change.

There were some attempts to discourage me from running for president of the AFL-CIO: "Not yet, John. We'll support you in the next go around." But I felt confident that I would have the support I needed. So I answered by saying, "I really think that I would be the best for instituting new programs in the AFL-CIO. I'll continue to work my ass off, after I'm elected, as I'm working right now. And I will continue to strive for your support."

I had some competition. Rich Trumka, the president of the United Mine Workers, who had a national reputation for strong leadership in difficult times, had been with our campaign for change from the beginning, and he had a lot of support. At age 45, he was the youngest member of the AFL-CIO's Executive Council and one of the most militant labor leaders around. But as it turned out, I had the support of the majority because the "dissidents," as the newspapers called us, wanted me to run for president and Rich to run for secretary-treasurer.

If I say so myself, we made a great team: there was no more loyal partner than Rich. And that team grew even stronger when Linda Chavez-Thompson agreed to run for the new position of executive vice president that we planned to establish at the upcoming AFL-CIO convention. At the time, Linda was a vice president of AFSCME and the only Latina member of the AFL-CIO Executive Council.

Once I emerged as the opposition candidate for the AFL-CIO presidency, it really was a battle. On June 28, we kicked off our campaign at a rally in downtown Washington, D.C., where I told the crowd I was running because America's working families needed a better deal. "I want to live in a country," I said, "where you can raise a family without having to hold down three jobs to do it. My idea of a just society is one in which honest labor raises the standard of living for all, rather than enormous wealth for a few." Linda said her message to our opponents in Congress and the boss's office was "No Más! Ya Basta! No more! We've had enough!" And Rich asked the crowd, which was cheering like crazy, "Why not a labor movement that's reaching out and winning over young workers and women workers, African Americans, Latinos, Asians?"

The "New Voice" Campaign. We called our campaign a New Voice for American Workers. The three of us were really very unified as a team. Our platform laid out an agenda for change: We wanted to organize at an unprecedented pace and scale. We wanted to build a more progressive political movement that can change workers' lives. We wanted to play an active role in the international labor movement to raise living standards all over the world. And finally, we wanted to lead a labor movement that speaks to and for all working families, unionized or not.

We worked our butts off to be successful. We were confident that we could win the election, based on the initial support that we had – something like 26 unions were behind us – and we trusted each other and confided in each other about the program and about any changes that we might consider after we were elected. But our whole focus was really on getting elected.

I accepted every invitation to speak that came my way. But we were listening, too, to what we heard from top leadership down to the thinking at the grassroots. People were very upbeat and optimistic. It was a new experience for the candidates for AFL-CIO office to have a contested election, a platform, and the intent to listen to every level of our labor movement. And people were impressed that to achieve greater diversity within the national leadership of the AFL-CIO, we were creating a new office of the executive vice president, and that officer was going to be a Latina woman, Linda Chavez-Thompson. Wherever we went, we would try to have opportunities with the media. We made sure that rank-and-file members knew that we wanted to hear them, their ideas and thoughts. We even published the campaign's phone number.

Debating My Differences with Tom Donahue. Around Labor Day of 1995, Frank Swoboda of the *Washington Post* reported on a debate that Tom Donahue and I had in Los Angeles, sponsored by the California Labor Federation. By this time, Lane had retired and Tom was serving as interim president. Swoboda started off his article with a description of the similarities between Tom and me. And we did have strong similarities: Both of us came out of SEIU, both had worked for the New York City building service union, Local 32B, and both of us had gone to Catholic colleges and learned a lot from Catholic labor priests. Furthermore, with our dark suits, neither of us looked like the change we were talking about.

But even if Swoboda could not see it, Tom and I were very different in many ways. That came out a few weeks later at another debate, this time in New York City, when we took the gloves off at the AFL-CIO convention. Tom said, "We have to worry less about blocking bridges and worry more about building bridges to the rest of society." And I replied that I was perfectly willing to build bridges, once the shelling stopped long enough for us to put up steel and pour concrete. "We need to be a full partner with our employers and full citizens of the communities we live in," I agreed. But I still believed in blocking bridges, I told the delegates, "whenever those employers or communities turn a deaf ear to the working families we represent."

Frankly, by that point, there was not too much that Tom and I disagreed on. In the end, he supported the same policy changes that I did, including a revitalization of our organizing and political programs. He did not agree with us, however, on the role of militant action and civil disobedience when necessary. Both our campaigns represented change in the AFL-CIO's status quo, but our New Voice campaign represented a significant change in attitude. As Linda Chavez-Thompson put it, "I like getting arrested for a good cause."

I always thought Tom Donahue made a major contribution to the AFL-CIO during Lane Kirkland's presidency, and I regret that this campaign brought an end to our friendship. He was a good friend and I was very much torn because on the one hand, I was confident I could win the election, and I was encouraged to run by a lot of the national union presidents. But it tore my heart, because I did not want to hurt Tom; he was a good friend. In the end, though, both of us thought the stakes were high and both of us did what we felt we had to do in the election.

Our Team Carries the Convention Vote. I truly believe that change is good for an organization, and at the 1995 AFL-CIO convention in New York City, a majority of the delegates agreed with me. It was not a walkover. Tom Donahue carried about 44 percent of the vote and I carried 56 percent. A larger number of unions supported Tom, but a larger number of members supported me. I was particularly grateful for the Operating Engineers' and the Laborers' support, since they brought a significant part of the building trades unions with them.

Our newly elected leadership team at the AFL-CIO's 1995 convention: (from left) Secretary-Treasurer Rich Trumka, Executive Vice President Linda Chavez-Thompson, and myself as president.

So we won. That was the upside. Now we had to prove that we could make a difference with our vision of devoting a greater part of the AFL-CIO's budget to organizing, diversifying the Executive Council by increasing it to 54 members (including 15 women or minority members), and improving and expanding grassroots political education and organizing. "As your president," I promised the convention, "I will never forget that our movement grows by addition and multiplication, not by division and subtraction."

Our campaign to bring a "New Voice" into the AFL-CIO rested on our ability to bring new attitudes, too. "We will use old-fashioned mass demonstrations as well as sophisticated corporate campaigns," I told the delegates, "to make workers' rights the civil rights issue of the 1990s." And to prove I was serious, one of my first official actions as the Federation's new president was to lead a march from the convention hotel to the garment district – where I got my start in the labor movement – to protest the sweatshop conditions that were making a comeback there.

A few days after my election, a reporter wondered whether a mild, quiet guy like me could really shake up the labor movement. I reminded him that many people thought I would be a "pussycat" when I took over the presidency of the SEIU. I told him, "My outward appearance may fool you. I hold strong beliefs that I am willing to fight hard to achieve." I pointed to my record at SEIU, where I had put together some of the most aggressive organizing campaigns in the country, built one of the most aggressive grassroots lobbying and political programs of any union, and doubled our membership. It boiled down to this: "I mean what I say: that is where the real fire is – doing the things I believe in, developing our programs, taking to the streets if need be, walking picket lines with our members during strikes."

That was the kind of leader I had been at SEIU – soft-spoken but militant, pragmatic but willing to take risks. And with the help of the AFL-CIO's new leadership team, that was the kind of AFL-CIO president I intended to be.

5

TAKING CHARGE AT THE AFL-CIO:
MY STRATEGY FOR CHANGE

I n my life I've made a few transitions: I've moved from the Bronx, to Yonkers, to the Washington, D.C., area, and from a staff position, to local union president, to the national head of SEIU. But assuming the presidency of the AFL-CIO in the fall of 1995 was a highly unique transition.

After all, the responsibilities are awesome, especially when you consider the diversity of the Federation's affiliates and the fact that you have to keep both the domestic situation and the international situation in mind. The president of the AFL-CIO deals with federal and state agencies and elected officials on all levels of government – including the president of the United States. He (or she) also deals with leaders of labor centers all around the world and international organizations like the International Labour Organization, the International Confederation of Free Trade Unions, the International Monetary Fund, and the World Bank. At the same time, there is the business of maintaining a good working relationship with the affiliates, individually and as a group, because the Federation can only be as successful as the affiliates are. The Federation really is a vehicle to help strengthen the affiliates – each having different experiences and challenges, different histories, and different sectors of the economy that they represent.

As a federation of strong affiliates, the AFL-CIO is a very complex bureaucracy. That was one of the biggest adjustments I had to make when I took over as AFL-CIO president. In that job, you are dealing with union presidents who were previously your peers, each with very strong ideas about what the Federation should be doing. I knew I had to strengthen my ties to the presidents, especially those selected to lead major AFL-CIO committees on issues like organizing or legislation. It was also important to reach out to their staff, the folks who ran their organizing and political programs. You can only be successful in the Federation if you have that kind of outreach and discussion.

Mandate for Change, from the Bottom Up. During the New Voice campaign I had talked about the need to grow: that if the AFL-CIO continued to represent only a small fraction of the workforce, we would never be able to win what we deserved at the bargaining table or in the legislative process. Now I was eager to strengthen the organizing program and the political program in particular and to improve relations with the individual affiliates. I was really looking forward to the opportunity to lead a large and strong Federation, and I intended to involve the affiliates in carrying out the mandates we had received at the convention through an active consultation process.

And I did actively involve the affiliates: in one of my first official actions, I appointed 70 representatives from 20 different unions to five working groups that analyzed the AFL-CIO's various departments and programs and came up with plans for changes. Later on, a Labor Council Advisory Committee, representing small, medium, and large labor councils from around the country, was also set up, to survey councils and then set priorities.

Our goal – that is, mine, Rich Trumka's, and Linda Chavez-Thompson's – had always been bigger than changing the leadership. We wanted to build a strong, new movement from the bottom up and to restore the voice of working Americans in their workplaces as well as their communities, their government, and the world economy. We had overcome the first hurdle, winning the election. Now we needed to take the next step: To motivate the affiliates and create the political will to invest in organizing the unorganized.

Creating a Culture of Organizing. For all of the heated debate at the 1995 AFL-CIO convention, the need to change was never the issue. The question was *how* to change. One of my first priorities for change was to rebuild a culture of organizing. The fact was, some affiliates had great organizing programs; some really did not have an organizing program at all; and some thought nothing of raiding a fellow union's members. Since the average local union spent less than 3 percent of its budget on organizing, I thought it was important for the AFL-CIO to get more involved in the process. After all, there were enough unorganized workers around the country to keep every affiliate pretty busy.

So our first step was expanding the Federation's capacity to organize. We established a new – actually the first – Organizing Department in January 1996, shifted $20 million into a new organizing "matching" fund to encourage national and local unions to launch strategic campaigns, and hired Richard Bensinger to direct the department. I wanted somebody who was experienced in organizing and who could train others, and Richard fit the bill. He had spent more than a decade organizing textile and clothing workers before he came to the AFL-CIO in 1989 to run the Organizing Institute. Since then he had been recruiting, training, and placing apprentice organizers, including recent college grads and community activists. As he described himself, Richard was part cheerleader, part ass-kicker, and part conscience, and he shared at least one virtue with his business opponents: He strongly believed in investing in growth.

But getting the majority of union members to share that belief was another question – and a very crucial one, because from Washington, D.C., the AFL-CIO can only pave the way. It was up to local and international unions to roll out the heavy artillery and redirect their resources into organizing. It would take something like $300 million a year just to stabilize our membership, and we certainly wanted to do more than just stand still. If we wanted to grow the way we needed to grow, dozens of international unions and tens of thousands of individual union members would have to say "count me in." They had to be willing to spend a larger part of their dues – say 20 to 30 percent – on building an organizing program. They would also have to be willing to take a broad view of their goals and work together in solidarity with other unions in their region or community, assisting all those workers who needed help.

Mobilizing with "Street Heat" and "Union Summer." To support the kind of joint organizing effort we were looking for, we were developing a strategy for rank-and-file mobilization, a rapid response system that we called "Street Heat." Workers took a pledge to respond wherever and however they were needed, at a street demonstration, a phone bank, a picket line, whatever. That way, whenever an employer was exploiting workers or overstepping the law to break an organizing campaign, the word would go out to tens of thousands of union members who were ready to take action – even if the battle belonged to another union; even if the workers involved were in another industrial sector; even if their skills were lower or their skin another color. That is the way we organize the unorganized. That is the way we bring the rights and respect of a union contract to our brothers and sisters who are suffering. And that is the way we rescue our unions, our families, and our futures: By putting the "movement" back into the labor movement.

In 1996 we were also trying to recruit a new generation of organizers. The Organizing Institute had a pretty good record of attracting college grads and community activists, but what about those who were still in school? Would it be possible to reach them? Labor organizing was a golden opportunity for young people who really wanted to make a difference. But unless they came from union families, they rarely heard anything positive about organized labor. To try and bridge that gap we launched a three-week internship program known as Union Summer. The name recalled the civil rights movement's Freedom Summer that had made such a difference in Mississippi in 1964. By giving college students a chance to see and participate in the labor movement as a social justice movement, and not the "special interest" portrayed in the media, we were investing in the future – ours and theirs.

The first year, more than 3,000 people from 45 states applied for Union Summer internships and 1,500 participated. They were really enthusiastic and did some serious work. In Los Angeles, they helped restaurant workers win union recognition. In Michigan, they helped drug store workers win a union contract. In St. Louis, they helped put a living wage referendum on the ballot. And overall, that first summer, they distributed more than 150,000 leaflets, made about 5,000 visits to workers in their homes, visited 1,500 work sites, and helped organize 235 protests and rallies, among other things. It was a good experience all around because the local unions liked having these kids. And the "Summeristas," as the interns called themselves, really got a lot out of the experience. They saw how hard it is to organize but they also learned that their hard work could really make a difference. They were seeing for themselves how small victories energized people to want and work for more.

Some of the interns took what they learned in the field back to school. They organized campus movements that led anti-sweatshop campaigns and living-wage campaigns, or they got involved with the collective bargaining process on campus, supporting cafeteria workers or other employees in their fight. So the Union Summer program had a broad impact.

We invited some of the Union Summer folks to an AFL-CIO Executive Council meeting to report on their activities. Five or six people came and spoke about their assignments and the different locals they worked with. One young woman who coordinated the report – a junior in college, I think – talked about her hopes that she would have a career in the labor movement when she graduated. She even thought that maybe someday she would like to be president of the AFL-CIO. So I just said, "That's really great – but not just yet." And everybody laughed.

New Grassroots Political Operations. Organizing and political action were my two greatest concerns as AFL-CIO president. So we were fighting two wars at once: We had to grow labor's ranks in order to have power at the polls, and we had to strengthen our clout in Washington to keep Congress from passing new laws that would make it even harder to organize and help working families. Ultimately, our strength depends on our members because the more members we have the more influence they have on the political process.

With 13 million members, the AFL-CIO was a formidable political force. The Christian Coalition, for instance, which backed the Republican Right, only had about 500,000 members at the time. Judging by the numbers, we should have had a better showing in the 1994 mid-term elections. It seemed to me and many others that we would have had better results if we had done a better job of informing our members about how their elected officials performed on issues like jobs, wages, Social Security, and Medicare – issues that mattered to them in their daily lives.

But our political strategy was about to change. The AFL-CIO was going to move beyond checkbook politics and top-down endorsements. Our politics had to start in the neighborhoods where our members lived and voted. We had to mobilize working men and women, whether they were union members or not, and build a movement that not only fought for, but listened to, the people it represented.

Our central message was one that just about every wage earner could support: "America Needs a Raise." Despite a pretty healthy economy, soaring profits on Wall Street, and rising productivity, the average wage was the lowest it had been in 40 years. People were working hard, but they were not getting ahead. They were getting frustrated and angry, especially when they saw executive compensation rise higher and higher – 400 percent in 20 years! So we had a unifying issue. But could we elect a labor-friendly Congress? Would they be willing to do something about the wage gap between the top 5 percent and the average worker, by raising the minimum wage? After all, it was only $4.25 at the time.

Thanks to global competition, downsizing, layoffs, and plant closings, working-class Americans and their families were hurting as never before. That meant we as the labor movement had to respond as never before. And I think we did.

To reestablish the AFL-CIO's political program as one of the nation's premier grassroots operations, we brought on Steve Rosenthal as political director. Steve had worked on political campaigns for the Communications Workers of America, he had been a top advisor to Clinton's Labor Secretary Robert Reich, and he had served as the deputy political director of the Democratic National Committee, running their 1992 coordinated campaign. He had the vision, the passion, and the experience to push us forward and build a powerful, progressive national movement of working people.

Next we put our money where our mouth was. The AFL-CIO Executive Council approved a 15 cent per capita assessment on our affiliates that raised a $35 million political war chest for a new political committee that we called Labor '96. Some of that money was spent to advertise the fact that Republicans were waging the worst assault on working families in 75 years. With AFSCME's Jerry McEntee as our leading strategist, we focused on issues like the minimum wage, Social Security, and Medicare, pointing out that Speaker of the House Newt Gingrich and his fellow Republicans were out of step with America.

One of our ads featured an elderly woman worried about Medicare funding, and then cut to Newt Gingrich saying, "We believe it's going to wither on the vine." An announcer came on to say, "They're going after Medicare again."

Ads like that really enraged some Republican candidates. In fact a couple of them came down to the AFL-CIO demanding that union TV ads running in their districts be pulled. When that did not work, they started airing their own attack ads, which showed an unflattering picture of me with the words "Union Boss" plastered across my forehead. So I guess our truth-telling hit a nerve. Perhaps it was not just our message that alarmed the Republicans, but the fact that we were holding elected officials accountable to working families.

We also started a National Labor Political Center to train activists, create educational materials for members, work with affiliates, and provide polling, research, and message development. We trained something like 2,500 union advocates to spread labor's message during the 1996 campaign; we placed over 100 coordinators in 86 congressional districts where we thought a strong labor vote could make a difference; we recruited over 10,000 volunteers to work on local campaigns. And for a real change of pace, we were working with groups like the Sierra Club and Citizen Action to block the Republicans' right-wing agenda that would dismantle a half-century of social advancement. We were coming together as a labor movement, educating workers on issues of importance to them, and expanding our registration and get-out-the-vote efforts. We were not only finding our voice, we were making it heard.

Our Message: America Needs a Raise! My job in revitalizing labor's political program was to take the message that "America Needs a Raise" on the road. The point was not just to stir up the crowds at rallies and meetings, although I certainly did a lot of that. It was to hear what working Americans had to say about how the current economic climate was affecting their everyday lives. So for about six weeks during the 1996 campaign, I traveled from coast to coast listening to stories of 70-hour work weeks, $3 an hour – and sometimes much less – pay, and sweatshop conditions that sounded more like 1896 than 1996. It was not just low-wage workers who were struggling. Middle-class construction managers, for instance, also had trouble paying their bills.

I went on the road across the country with my "America Needs a Raise" organizing blitz; as seen here with Local 100 in Houston, 1996.

We listened to testimony from working and retired and unemployed and disabled women and men in 30 cities. Each city was different, but every story was the same: Over and over, hard-working Americans shared their anger about long hours and low pay, their fears that global competition put them and their families in an economic race to the bottom, and their sense that employers held all the cards. They felt powerless because they had no voice at work: They knew from experience that if they objected to the conditions on their job or were unsatisfied with their wages, someone was always ready to replace them. These workers were running out of money, running out of options, and running out of hope. That is a dangerous combination, because when people feel powerless, when they believe that no one is fighting for their right to a secure future, they tend to blame scapegoats, like immigrants or minority workers. And that is when democracy is in real trouble.

These workers' stories demonstrated in all-too-human terms that the social contract that defined the American Dream for much of the 20th century – that workers are entitled to a fair share of the wealth they produce – was broken. A rising tide no longer lifted all boats. Instead we saw a growing gap between the rich and the rest of us. That was the point I emphasized in countless newspaper interviews, television appearances, and public discussions. I did not pull any punches. At the America Needs a Raise rally on Wall Street, for example, I asked a couple of pointed questions: If corporate profits were up 200 percent, why were working families' incomes down 12 percent? If productivity was up 24 percent, and the stock market up over 400 percent, why were working families running out of money and running out of hope? And if the upcoming election was all about family values, why were moms and dads working three jobs just to stay even, leaving no time to spend with their kids?

The answer seemed pretty clear to me. "Because for the past 20 years, Wall Street and corporate America have been putting profits before people," I told the crowd that was gathered on Wall Street. "Because for the past 20 years, the politicians we send to Washington have been pandering to the rich and the big corporations and pounding on the middle class and the poor.

Because for the past 20 years, American workers have been worked like mules and treated like dogs, left out and shut out of decisions affecting their jobs, and because they've been fired, laid off, riffed, outsourced, temporarily replaced, permanently replaced, downsized, right-sized, marginalized and ostracized from the very society they built with their sweat and blood."

It did not have to be this way. To Wall Street, I said, "Stop rewarding CEOs who run their companies into the ground by running workers into the unemployment line." To corporate America, I said, "Start exporting products instead of jobs, start consulting your employees when it comes to productivity, quality, and competitiveness, start paying them enough to afford the goods and services they produce." To government, I said, "Stop raising taxes on the middle class and the working poor, stop giving tax breaks to the wealthy and the big corporations, stop the Wall Street wizards who are gambling away our future, and *stop stalling around on the minimum wage!*" Otherwise, I said, the AFL-CIO and its allies would "agitate and educate and march and strike until American workers and their families *get a raise!*"

The campaign drew a lot of attention and support. Public opinion was on our side, and that brought politicians from Bill Clinton, to Bob Dole, to Pat Buchanan along, too. As I heard our friend Senator Tom Harkin put it: "America Needs a Raise. Donald Trump doesn't." (Keep in mind this was in 1996!) So we were making progress. By the time the Democratic convention met in Chicago in August, President Clinton had already signed legislation that raised the minimum wage by 90 cents an hour over the next year, a raise that benefited some 10 million men and women. But that was just a start as far as we were concerned: We still had billboard trucks weaving through the streets of Chicago spreading the message that "America Needs a Raise."

Here we are taking our fight for an increase in the minimum wage to Capitol Hill, with a rally on the Capitol steps.

It was important to me that we not only publicize workers' economic fears and frustrations but also offer some solutions. So with the help of David Kusnet, the former chief speech writer for Bill Clinton, I incorporated what we learned into a book, *America Needs a Raise: Fighting for Economic Security and Social Justice*. When it was published on Labor Day 1996 – to pretty good reviews, I am happy to say, and a burst of positive publicity – the book helped activate those interested in our campaign.

Labor's Working Capital. Closely related to the issue of wages was the question of workers' pension, health, and welfare plans, and whether the capital held by these plans was being invested to support workers' goals for economic security and social justice. These pension and benefit plans manage trillions of dollars of workers' hard-earned income – earnings that workers have chosen, through collective bargaining, to set aside to finance their retirement and health benefits. It is their capital, and it has real economic power on Wall Street. But we could see that too often, that capital was invested against the economic interests of working families. We asked why workers' capital should be invested in the stock of companies that were known for exploiting their employees, violating labor laws, or exporting American jobs overseas. Workers have every right to expect that the capital they have put aside for their pensions and health and welfare benefits will work for them, not against them.

Soon after taking office I established the AFL-CIO Center for Working Capital to spearhead our capital stewardship efforts and give workers a greater voice in the use of these funds. Secretary-Treasurer Rich Trumka headed up this work. We took steps to educate the labor trustees who serve on the boards of their pension and benefit plans, so they could speak up more knowledgeably in advocating for responsible investing. We wanted them to understand that when trustees are considering investments of equal economic value to their fund, they are allowed to select the investments that best support working families and their communities. Rich directed a detailed study of investment vehicles available to pension and benefit plans, and we ranked them according to how well the investment strategies aligned with union values and whether they were prudent stewards of workers' capital. Rich, Linda, and I had the opportunity to serve on the boards of several of the high-performing labor-friendly funds. Among these were the AFL-CIO Housing Investment Trust and AFL-CIO Building Investment Trust as well as ULLICO's J for Jobs, all of which had strong records of using labor's capital to create union jobs, promote community development, and strengthen the neighborhoods where union families live and work while earning competitive returns.

We also undertook a campaign to promote sound corporate governance and increase corporate accountability to our communities. As part of this, we focused on increasing worker representation on corporate boards, and on educating our pension and health plan trustees about voting their shares of corporate stock in accordance with workers' economic interests. These capital strategies have done a great deal to support the goals and priorities of working families.

Political and Organizing Work in Progress. In 1996, a year after I took over as president, our political program was still a work in progress. Despite all our hard work, labor-friendly candidates failed to take over the House. I was not discouraged, though. After all, Bill Clinton was reelected, 18 Republican Congressmen would not be returning, and the percentage of union voters had increased, along with the percentage of our members voting Democratic. We were also encouraged because candidates on both sides of the aisle had focused on our issues – Medicare, the minimum wage, education spending, and health insurance portability. So the AFL-CIO did influence the agenda. Our political push had roused labor into action, proving that we were once again a powerful player on the national scene. Republicans had criticized the money we spent – they claimed it was $100 million, a gross exaggeration. I thought our $35 million was money well spent.

Our organizing program was another work in progress – and it was clear more progress needed to be made. Polls told us that women represented labor's future: They were more pro-union, more inclined to collective action, more collaborative, and more likely to side with the union against management during a fight. But they were often employed in minimum wage or part-time work, so we needed more than the traditional organizing approach.

That is why we hired Karen Nussbaum, SEIU's former colleague at District 925, to head the AFL-CIO's newly established Working Women's Department. We hired her away from the Department of Labor, where she had served with distinction as director of the Women's Bureau. She was the right person for our women's organizing project and proved it with the "Ask a Working Woman" survey and conferences that followed. These legendary meetings brought together women from the labor movement, the civil rights movement, and religious and community organizations for some very enlightening discussions. She knew that we would not achieve justice in the workplace or society without the involvement and the leadership of working women. She also knew, and was able to persuade others, that issues like equal pay, child care, family leave, and flexible time were not just important to women, but to the movement as a whole.

Building Local Capacity with "Union Cities." Another important hire was Marilyn Sneiderman, who came on as director of Field Mobilization, a department that worked hand-in-hand with the Organizing Department. Her task was to streamline the AFL-CIO's field operation from 12 regional offices to four, with a coordinator in every state, and work with some 600 central labor councils to organize and build community alliances. The idea was to strengthen our community roots so that we could organize new workers, win better contracts, elect labor allies to public office, and get better laws passed.

Union Cities is the name we gave our new program to strengthen the labor councils and their capacity for doing organizing and political work. It grew out of a meeting we had with 150 labor council representatives, which had led to a survey of over 300 councils. That survey told us a lot about how local leaders thought their councils should function. The most effective labor councils, we learned, did a lot of education on economic issues, involved their members in plenty of "street heat," and made a real effort to promote people of color and women to leadership positions.

So we developed a kind of road map – a "guide to greatness," as the Field Mobilization Department put it – for developing the kind of labor movement that could really speak for working families. Local councils that wanted to be part of the Union Cities program had to make a real commitment: They had to persuade affiliates to shift resources into organizing; one percent of their membership had to sign up for Street Heat; and they had to organize political action committees to build community support for labor issues and labor-oriented candidates. Union Cities councils also had to organize community alliances to promote job growth and family-friendly community standards for local industry and public investments; they had to sponsor the AFL-CIO's education program, Common Sense Economics; and they had to promote diversity among their officers, committees, delegates, and other positions.

It was a pretty ambitious plan, and not every council sought the designation. But most of them were working towards those goals. Generally speaking, the results were encouraging, because the more the local councils mobilized their members for political action, multi-trade organizing campaigns, strike support, and community-based activities, the more the members wanted to participate. I think some council leaders were really surprised to see how active their members wanted to be and how willing they were to move forward, once they had an opportunity to act.

Using what we learned with Union Cities, we would later go on to establish the New Alliance program to bring new unity and vitality to the state federations.

Thinking Globally. With Union Cities, we were making a real effort to act locally, but as a movement, we were also trying to think globally, as the saying goes. Given the fact of multinational corporations and international competition, our new leadership team could not ignore the larger world. But how to engage it was another question, and a sensitive one, since there were still some hard feelings about how Lane Kirkland had handled international affairs. Part of that was resolved when we consolidated the controversial, Cold War oriented foreign policy institutes of the Meany-Kirkland era into a single organization, the American Center for International Labor

Solidarity, better known as the Solidarity Center. We shifted the emphasis from containing communism to promoting international solidarity for the enforcement of workers' rights, especially the right to organize. In all our discussions, we talked about how we could work in a more coordinated way and advocate for workers' rights all over the world.

People knew that as president of SEIU I had gotten the union very involved in international affairs. I had recommended that SEIU affiliate with FIET, the International Federation of Commercial, Clerical and Technical Employees (now known as UNI, the Union Network International). Lane Kirkland had appointed me as a delegate to the International Labour Organization in the 1980s, where I got an opportunity to talk with representatives of the major powers within the labor movement, from Great Britain, France, Germany, Italy, and Canada. I had also served on the ILO's working group on safety and health issues, a subject in which I was very interested. That all proved to be very useful now that I was AFL-CIO president and it paved the way for my later work with TUAC, the Trade Union Advisory Committee, and the OECD, the Organisation for Economic Co-operation and Development. [4]

Now as the AFL-CIO's new president, my major international task, as I saw it, was to build a strong, international movement to counter the harmful consequences of globalization. We wanted to work with unions in the developing countries to support a common program that considered workers' rights and environmental protections, as well as a corporation's costs and profits. Our position was that while we did not believe that free markets were necessarily fair, we did not have our heads in the sand, either. We were ready to embrace the global market, as long as trade agreements guaranteed the protections we sought for worker's rights and the environment. As things stood, trade agreements were primarily concerned with protecting the rights of capital. As far as labor was concerned, the question was not whether we were internationalists, but what values our internationalism served.

Labor's Values in the Global Marketplace. We were successful in 1997 in fighting Bill Clinton's request for fast-track authority in negotiating trade agreements, a process that allows no amendments and limits debate on trade deals like NAFTA. But the fight did not stop there. We had to keep pressing the point that trade agreements without workers' rights, human rights, and environmental standards undermined wages and jobs throughout the world – not just in the U.S.

That would be an argument I continued to make throughout my time at the AFL-CIO, because international trade institutions like the World Trade Organization, or WTO, still opposed linking labor standards to trade. So whether I was addressing Congress, or the Council on Foreign Relations, the International Labour Organization, or the State Department, I spread the word that new rules were necessary to make the global marketplace work for working people.

There were some people who argued that "workers' rights" was a Western concept and we did not understand the benefits of free trade to developing nations. But frankly, no society benefits from exploiting its children rather than educating them, and no society benefits from impoverishing its working men and women rather than empowering them. Not ours and not theirs.

Marching on the WTO in Seattle. Our most successful effort to connect the issues of globalization, workers' rights, and social justice grew out of the World Trade Organization's decision to hold a meeting in Seattle in 1999. The WTO is the capstone of the corporate-dominated world market. It oversees and enforces the rules of the global economy, arbitrates trade conflicts, and claims the authority to challenge state and national laws that conflict with its rules – rules that protect corporate, not human, interests.

For instance, when voters in Massachusetts wanted to boycott companies doing business with the slave labor regime in Burma, they were told that a boycott would violate the WTO's trade accord.

The Seattle meeting was supposed to launch a new round of trade agreements. But that is not what happened, thanks to tens of thousands of working people from the United States and scores of other countries who decided to march and rally in Seattle. A broad coalition of union members, environmentalists, consumer activists, and other citizens' groups – some called us the "greenie-Sweeney alliance" – were united in our call to the WTO to review its record and reform its rules before taking on new areas for negotiations. As I told the crowd at a rally, our demands were simple and clear: We wanted prohibitions against child labor and slave labor and we wanted workers to have the right to organize unions. We wanted enforceable rules to incorporate environmental and consumer protections. And we wanted negotiations to be more transparent so that citizens could have a voice. We were not going to wait for the WTO to act, either. What we were doing in Seattle, I said loud and clear, was the beginning of a fight that had to be brought to every level of government in every country around the world. And then I said, "Let's march!"

A Demonstration of Solidarity. Our Field Mobilization Department had started planning in August of 1999 to mobilize union members from Vancouver to San Francisco for the November march in Seattle, working with all the central labor councils, state federations, and local unions in the region. It was a complicated job, setting up transportation, housing, parking, parade routes, and all the rest. Fortunately the King County Labor Council in Washington and the Vancouver Labor Council in British Columbia were well organized "Union Cities," so we had plenty of help. Everybody seemed to realize what a great opportunity this was for the labor movement to work together.

Our major affiliates with strong feelings on trade issues, like the Steelworkers, the Machinists, and the Auto Workers, or on human rights issues, like SEIU, were early supporters. So the turnout for the rally was good, and the march around Seattle was great. In fact it turned out to be the largest public protest in Seattle's history, bringing together 40,000 people in a common goal. Local officials were naturally wary of so many people eager to demonstrate, but we were able to reach an agreement on where we could march and where we could gather, and we stuck to it.

One image stands out in my mind. When we got as close as we could get to the convention center, where the actual trade meeting was going on, we all knelt down on the street to pray for the trade ministers inside. I still have the picture. To see me with James Hoffa from the Teamsters, Leo Gerard from the Steelworkers, and Steve Yokich from the UAW, to see seven or eight of us in the first line, kneeling down praying, well, we do not come together to pray very often. It was a very moving experience for me.

Despite what the papers reported, there was no rioting in Seattle. But there were sporadic episodes of violence and vandalism, such as a brick going through a McDonald's window, and we did not encourage or excuse any of that. There was a band of self-styled "anarchists" from nearby Eugene, Oregon, who did not believe in rules of any kind, and they were responsible for most of the damage that occurred. I was struck by the irony. Here we had a handful of local anarchists looting and pillaging in Seattle, while the rest of us were peacefully protesting the actions of another group of anarchists, global anarchists, the multinational corporations that were looting and pillaging entire societies and did not want any rules to get in their way.

When we got to the end of the march, I walked back to our hotel with a few others, mostly international people. The police were all around us. I remember stopping at a traffic light to let the next unit of marchers through. The light then turned green for us; it turned red for the marchers, and the marchers stopped. One of the guys from Great Britain said, "God almighty, I can't believe it. I never saw anarchists stop for a traffic light." I had to laugh. Although the newspapers were calling us anarchists, our march and the demonstrations that followed, as well as countless actions by thousands of young people, were peaceful.

It was a momentous week, to say the least. Our march and the heightened scrutiny that went with it made it impossible for trade negotiators to conduct business as usual. There would be no papering over differences and passing off a bad deal as acceptable. In fact, there would be no deal at all, because the WTO talks in Seattle simply collapsed. It was not exactly a victory, because we did not get the rules on human rights and worker rights that we wanted. But in this case, as I said all that week, no deal was better than a bad deal.

President Clinton's Breakthrough Support. While all this was going on, I had the opportunity to meet with President Bill Clinton. He was going to give a major address to all the WTO delegates, and he asked me to come and sit down in his suite, so he could advise me of his take on the meeting. I was not sure what to expect. The president, after all, had negotiated a trade deal with China – a country where anyone attempting to organize a union was immediately arrested and imprisoned; that agreement would potentially bring China into the WTO. The administration believed that it would be easier to achieve reforms that way, but we thought it was a grave mistake, and I did not hesitate to let the president know that. Whether he feared how this would affect our enthusiasm for Vice President Gore's 2000 presidential campaign, or whether the strength of a labor-environmental-human rights coalition gave him pause, I do not know. But at our meeting in Seattle, the president told me that he was going to be a strong advocate for making workers' rights a part of the trade agreement, even though that meant the failure of the talks he wanted so much to succeed.

He kept his word. President Clinton not only pressed our demands for the protections we sought, and for a work group to get the process started, but he shook the WTO to its core with his statement supporting economic sanctions for trading nations that violated fundamental freedoms. The sound of marching feet had toughened his position that week. So if the Battle in Seattle did not produce a change in WTO policy, it did produce a breakthrough in the debate, at least. As a nation, we had crossed the threshold to begin a serious conversation about rules, standards, and values in the global economy. And we did not intend to let up on our efforts. We were in it for the long haul.

AFL-CIO at the End of 1990s: Road to Recovery. Looking back over our experiences in the 1990s, we certainly felt that the AFL-CIO was on the road to recovery. Our affiliates had organized some 400,000 new members in 1998 and we counted a net increase of 250,000 members by 1999 – not nearly enough, of course, but we were headed in the right direction. In Las Vegas, a multi-trade campaign to organize hotel workers, hospital workers, and construction workers was certainly encouraging. The Laborers there grew by 50 percent, the Carpenters added 2,000 new members, and the Roofers union grew from 80 to 800 members. The Las Vegas campaign did not go as far as I had hoped – some union presidents really needed to put the fear of God into reluctant local leaders, because it seemed to me that many of the problems that arose were really resolvable. But it was a good example of what can be achieved when unions in different sectors join forces to move forward with organizing.

We had had our ups and our downs. On the one hand, our efforts to support farm workers through our "Strawberry Campaign" in California, while dramatic and inspiring, did not achieve the success we were hoping for, although we did demonstrate the AFL-CIO's willingness to directly support organizing campaigns. On the other hand, we had better success – and drew widespread publicity – when we supported the Teamsters' strike at UPS over the hardships caused by part-time work, part-time pay, and few benefits. We not only proved that the AFL-CIO would go to bat for low-wage workers, but that we could still win a national fight.

Of course, we were not done changing, yet: We established the Voice@Work campaign to address – and expose – the widespread suppression of the right to organize. This campaign was directed by Arlene Holt Baker, an experienced and talented leader from AFSCME who was working in my office as assistant to the president. Voice@Work brought grassroots organizers together with community activists to build support for organizing campaigns and labor law reform and to make the right to organize recognized as a basic human and civil right. In 1998, more than 10,000 workers and activists in 70 cities had participated in "A Day to Make Our Voices Heard." With Arlene's help in 1999, we expanded those activities to cover an entire week. So in a sense, the Voice@Work campaign was part "America Needs a Raise" and part "Justice for Janitors," focusing community attention on the faces and stories of working families in order to change – and improve – employer behavior.

In the meantime, our plans to revitalize our political power at the grassroots level were going strong. Through a new group called Scholars, Artists, and Writers for Social Justice, we were reconnecting with allies in the church, in the civil rights, women's, and environmental movements, and even with intellectuals. These alliances were paying off. In over 30 states, including California, we helped to defeat anti-labor legislation like so-called "paycheck protection" laws that attempted to limit political fundraising by public employee unions.

And we had a pretty successful election season in 1998. Despite the president's well-publicized personal problems, we picked up five seats in the House, held onto the Senate, and had the pleasure of seeing Newt Gingrich step down as Speaker of the House, and then drop out of Congress entirely.

Another important milestone of change came in February 2000, when the AFL-CIO Executive Council adopted a resolution that put us squarely on the side of immigrant workers, whether they had documents or not. As the son of immigrants, I was particularly proud of this change of heart. The newest immigrants might not share the same skin color or background as my Irish immigrant parents, but they faced many of the same problems. Our new immigration policy would lead to a partnership agreement in 2006 with the National Day Laborer Organizing Network, an umbrella organization for over 40 worker centers that were focused on protecting day laborers' rights on the job and giving them a public voice in the community. This historic partnership promised to benefit both organizations. By accessing the AFL-CIO's extensive legislative and policy-making experience, the worker centers would have a better chance to translate local victories into lasting improvements; and by accessing the worker centers' strong ties to the immigrant community, AFL-CIO unions and labor councils would be in a stronger position to expose abuses and improve workplace standards in a variety of hard-to-organize industries. That gave us all a lot of hope.

Storms on the Horizon. I think it is fair to say that we had good reasons to be optimistic as we entered the new century. We had new structures in place to mobilize our ranks, but we could not claim to command the support of all our affiliates all the time. There were still many union leaders who resented the AFL-CIO's "interference," particularly where organizing was concerned. And while we had certainly improved labor's public face and drew far more respectful headlines in mainstream publications like *Time*, we did weather an ugly storm when Teamsters President Ron Carey was implicated in a fund-raising scandal and was forced to step down.

As disheartening as that episode was, it did not compare to the storm that was on the horizon. Because by the time we were proudly marching with the movement to legalize undocumented immigrants in May 2001, we had a new – and decidedly unfriendly – U.S. president, George W. Bush, to contend with. "Now you will know how bad those people are," Lane Kirkland's widow, Irena, said to me at an AFL-CIO function soon after the election. "Now you will know what Lane went through with Bush Senior." Believe me, she was not kidding.

6

TWO STEPS FORWARD, ONE STEP BACK: NEW CHALLENGES

Five years into my leadership of the AFL-CIO, organizing remained our number one priority. And for the first time in a long time, we felt like the time was right to move forward on the legal front. The stock market was soaring, employment was strong, and political currents seemed to be moving in the right direction. "Labor '98," our grassroots campaign, had helped reduce the Republican majority, and our "2000 in 2000" campaign saw the election of more than 400 union members out of about 600 union candidates running for local office. That progress raised some tantalizing questions: What if we had more members? What if we created a seamless web of legislative, political, and organizing activity to defend the rights of workers to form or join unions and to help transform new members into a bigger union movement and a stronger political force?

I say tantalizing because U.S. labor law was not on our side, a fact that made our goal that much harder to reach. And the general public was unaware of the problem. Our experience launching our Voice@Work campaign made it very clear that everyday citizens did not understand how limited workers' rights are under U.S. labor law. They might have heard of the National Labor Relations Act, or NLRA, and its promise to protect workers' rights to organize and promote collective bargaining. But they did not realize that that promise had been broken long ago.

The Failures of Existing Labor Law. To say that U.S. labor law is stacked against employees who want to organize a union is putting it mildly. Because the fact is, many employers intimidate and coerce workers not to unionize, either by firing activists or threatening to shut the company down. They get away with it even though both behaviors are illegal under NLRA rules. And employers can easily nullify the right to strike: They simply replace the striking workers permanently. To top things off, employers can even nullify an election that does not go their way. Look at what happened to the metal trades workers employed by Avondale Industries, the largest nonunion shipyard in the United States. A majority of those workers voted for a union in 1993 but they could not claim their victory. Over the next six years, management fired union activists, intimidated the workforce, and spent more than $2 million (which Avondale then billed to its largest customer, the U.S. Navy) to keep the case tied up in court. The workers were never permitted to negotiate their union contract.

Unfortunately, this was not an exceptional case or even a new story. When the Dunlop Commission on the Future of Worker-Management Relations made its report back in 1994, it found that one out of four employers illegally fired union activists during organizing campaigns, and one out of 10 activists lost their jobs. The Commission concluded: "The U.S. is the only major democratic country in which the choice of whether or not workers are to be represented by a union is subject to such a controversial process." Six years later, the picture was not any brighter. After a year-long study of workers employed in a variety of industries all over the country, Human Rights Watch, an independent international organization, concluded that U.S. workers lack the most fundamental, internationally recognized human rights at the workplace – the basic freedom to organize, bargain, and strike.

So this was not a new problem, and it was not an easy one to resolve, either. The last time the AFL-CIO had attempted a national campaign to reform labor law, when Jimmy Carter was president, we could not line up enough votes in the Senate to overcome an anti-reform filibuster. And then we had to give up the idea of labor law reform, given the bleak political outlook.

As we approached the 2000 election campaign, though, the forecast for labor reform looked a little brighter. We needed to win six Senate seats, six House seats, and six "battleground" union-friendly states to elect an all-around Democratic administration headed by Al Gore, our candidate for president. Although his position on trade could have been better, there was no doubt in my mind as to where he stood on the right to organize. Al Gore was, in my estimation, the most outspoken champion of the freedom to join a union since Franklin Delano Roosevelt and our best hope to even the playing field where the National Labor Relations Act was concerned.

We did not think that labor law reform would magically improve our ability to organize overnight. Some problems would remain, whether the law was changed or not: problems such as the U.S. economy's shift to service work from manufacturing, the pressure of global competition, and the still very critical need to convince some of our affiliates to go out and organize. But we would certainly get a boost if we got the labor law reforms we were asking for: card check recognition, which was a simpler way to organize a union; first contract arbitration, to insure that workers organizing a union actually got a union contract; enforceable penalties for illegal behavior; an end to striker replacement; and the expansion of NLRA coverage for domestic workers, agricultural workers, and workers misclassified as independent contractors. In the meantime our reform campaign would educate workers about the value of a union and educate the public about the difficulties workers face when they try to unionize.

The Disastrous Presidential Election of 2000. Our plan for labor law reform was based on a big assumption: That our friend Al Gore would defeat George W. Bush in the 2000 presidential election and would help us pass this legislation.

We all know that did not happen. But it was not for our lack of trying. We had some 1,600 workers coordinating voter education programs in 35 states; we registered 2.3 million new union household voters; we spent $6 million on grassroots activities to mobilize African American and Latino voters. And we did help Al Gore win the popular vote. Even the *Wall Street Journal* noticed that union households made the crucial difference in some important swing states. But it is the Electoral College vote that matters, and George W. Bush, with the help of the Supreme Court, managed to win that.

Overall, it was a very tough campaign. Our opponents in the Chamber of Commerce had definitely stepped up their game with a well-financed grassroots campaign of their own. The National Rifle Association also had a very successful ad campaign with their message: "Don't risk having President Gore take away your gun." A lot of union members hunt, so guns were a big issue. We countered with: "Al Gore doesn't want to take away your gun. But George W. Bush wants to take away your union." Unfortunately, a number of union hunters were not persuaded, which caused some regret over the next few years. As one of them put it, "I voted my gun, then they picked my pocket."

We were not happy with the election outcome, and we did not pretend to be happy with the way it was achieved. As far as I was concerned, the Supreme Court's decision to stop recounting the ballots in Florida and award them to George W. Bush ignored the fundamental principle of "one person, one vote," and profoundly threatened the faith of citizens in our democracy and our system of justice. But despite those grave flaws in the voting process, the AFL-CIO did not have much choice but to work with President Bush. As I told the press, we were willing to cooperate to bring our nation together and address the many important concerns of America's working men and women. I assumed that the president would be open to such cooperation, but that turned out to be the wrong assumption.

Reaching Out to the Bush White House. Having had the experience of leading a union through the Reagan administration, I knew the going would be tough. But Ronald Reagan at least tried to deal with people on the other side, like Speaker of the House Tip O'Neill. So I expected some give-and-take, and to get started on the right foot, I made the obligatory phone call to congratulate the president-elect. The labor movement has always been civil in dealing with whoever was elected president and offering congratulations, Democrat or Republican. I made the call after the Supreme Court decided the election, which was during the second week of December.

I did not get any response to that call until the week between Christmas and New Year's, when I was in New York City celebrating the holidays with my family. My office got a call from the White House, and they tracked me down at my hotel. Andy Card, the president's chief of staff, said that the president was anxious to talk to me, and that they apologized for not getting back to me sooner. Somehow my phone message had fallen between the cracks, Card said, and somebody thought that it was from a different John Sweeney: the Republican congressman from upstate N.Y.

President-elect Bush was very cordial, thanking me for the congratulations and saying he wanted to have a decent relationship. He said he wanted to have dialogue and talk about the issues. I assured him, "That's what we want as well. We've talked to every president, whether he's Republican or Democrat. We had these conversations with your father."

The president said that he agreed and he would try to get opportunities to talk. The call lasted about seven or eight minutes. That was the last time I spoke to him.

President Bush was less engaged than his father. He did not really want a dialogue on worker and social issues. His father, President George H. W. Bush, showed a measure of civility in dealing with Congress and gave the appearance of wanting to work some things out. The son, however, did not. I think that Karl Rove, who was senior advisor to President Bush at the time, was calling the shots. We knew where President Bush stood on labor issues and on progressive issues, but I did not think our relations would be as bad as they turned out to be.

For the record, I did visit the Bush White House in 2008 when Pope Benedict XVI visited that spring. But I considered that to be at the invitation of the Pope, not the President. I regret the disappearance of the old bipartisan relationships that used to be an essential part of the political process in Washington.

Nominees for Secretary of Labor. President Bush announced his first candidate for secretary of labor, Linda Chavez, who had held positions in the Reagan and senior Bush administrations. We were opposed to the nomination because we knew what her philosophy was. She was outspoken in opposing so many issues that were important to us. She wrote an occasional column in the newspaper, she did TV programs. And she took a very strong stand against the minimum wage, which was one of the most important issues to us. I said to Rich Trumka and Linda Chavez-Thompson that we should really set up an interview session as we would do with any prospective secretary of labor.

We had her come over to the AFL-CIO one morning a couple of days after she was nominated. We were in a conference room right outside my office, and she was on one side of the table and we were on the other side. I started off by just saying, "I know your position is clear on some issues that are labor issues, but I guess none stands out more than the minimum wage. Is there any hope that your position would change on the minimum wage when you become secretary?" And she made it clear that she would not be changing her position and that was how her position would stand. So I thanked her for coming over. I said, "I don't think that there is much that we can talk about that will have any influence on you, and we just shouldn't waste each other's time."

Not long after that, her name was withdrawn. Apparently she had harbored an undocumented immigrant in her home for a number of years, which did not sit well with the Bush administration. So I took the opportunity to put in a call to Andy Card at the White House. I told him that I hoped that we would have an opportunity to discuss whoever the president was considering next for labor secretary. I said, "It can be a couple of names, whatever, but just allow us to give you a rundown on where we think these people stand." Within an hour or so, Card got back to me and told me the president was ready to announce his choice, someone "who says that she has a good relationship with you." He was reluctant to release the name, Elaine Chao, thinking that I was going to hold a press conference or something.

"Well," I said, "Elaine Chao has led the United Way and I've been on the board of the United Way." Then Card said she had also been on the board of Northwest Airlines and the airline unions have had decent relationships with her. "And she says you and she get along very well."

"Well, I don't know. If she means about the weather . . ." and we both had a laugh.

After Secretary Chao was confirmed, I was invited to her installation. She held a reception in her office, just greeting people. So I got on the reception line. There was one other labor officer, James P. Hoffa, president of the Teamsters. So I chatted with him for a while.

Senator Mitch McConnell of Kentucky, who was Elaine Chao's husband, was standing in the wings, and I went over and shook hands with him. He then sent one of his staff over to talk to me, and he asked if I could meet with the senator to talk about the campaign finance bill. I said, "Sure, I'll be happy to. I can come to the senator's office tomorrow."

So the next morning I went over with Larry Gold, the attorney who was working with us on campaign finance. As we walked into the office, Senator McConnell said, "Thanks for coming over. I guess you probably have similar thoughts as I have. I never thought I'd have the president of the AFL-CIO in my office, and I guess you probably are thinking that you never thought that you'd come to the office of McConnell."

"I think you got that right," I said.

We talked about some specifics in the campaign finance bill. Larry asked him some technical questions, and someone from his staff did call Larry the next day to discuss the legislation. But that was the last conversation I had with Mitch McConnell.

Uneven Organizing Efforts by Affiliates. I have often said, "Labor must organize without the law so that we can later organize under the law." But unfortunately that was not happening.

We thought we had turned a crucial corner in 1999, when we posted the highest net membership increase in 10 years. But we still were not moving ahead: At the turn of the 21st century, union density fell to 13.5 percent of the workforce, the lowest point in 60 years. The American economy was growing strongly and millions of new jobs were being created. But they tended to be nonunion jobs because the workforce was growing in industries and occupations where unions were weakest. Jobs were expanding in the hard-to-organize service sector, in retail, finance, advertising, health care, and new information technologies, for instance, while union manufacturing jobs were being moved overseas. Construction was booming in some markets, but those markets tended to be in the South or Southwest, or in the suburbs of major cities, where unionization had never been strong. If we could not organize quickly in these growing industries and population centers, as I told the Executive Council, we would not be a viable institution for long, and then we would not be able to make any impact on the issues we cared about.

The AFL-CIO was doing what I thought we should be doing – creating a climate for change to motivate the membership, training organizers, providing support for strategic campaigns, and so forth. But frankly, I had far more success persuading affiliates to become politically active than I did persuading them to step up their organizing campaigns. That was a major problem because it is not the Federation that files petitions for union representation elections or signs up new members. Affiliates have that responsibility. And only a few took it seriously. Around 10 affiliates were doing 80 percent of the organizing. And that aggravated some of the most active union leaders who thought the AFL-CIO should be doing more than providing assistance and training. Some thought that instead of trying to build a consensus for organizing, I should have been forcing affiliates to get busy or get out of the way.

Carpenters Leave the AFL-CIO. Doug McCarron, the president of the Carpenters, brought the issue of our organizing program to a head when he led his union out of the AFL-CIO in March 2001. He was pretty proud of the fact that, under his leadership, the Carpenters had become one of the fastest growing unions. Their membership increased from around 325,000 in 1995 to around 500,000 by 2001. McCarron had centralized authority for organizing in the international union, and although some members questioned his methods, since their local unions had lost their autonomy, as far as he was concerned, his top-down approach to organizing was the way to go. He wanted the rest of the affiliates to follow his lead and spend half of their budgets on organizing. McCarron thought the AFL-CIO was spending too much money on staff, too little on organizing, and was too protective of the affiliates' rights to set their own organizing budgets. One of the reasons he gave for disaffiliating was that the AFL-CIO "continues to operate under the rules and procedures of an era that passed years ago."

I was not completely surprised. I had had discussions with Doug McCarron over a period of time. We talked very frankly about the Federation. But for the most part, his concerns were related to the construction industry, particularly the question of trade jurisdiction. The Carpenters had a long history of jurisdictional fights with the Sheet Metal Workers and the Iron Workers, among many others, so there was plenty of bad blood there. And I understood that. If there was anything that got my blood pressure up, it was when a union just came in and raided your members, not respecting the AFL-CIO's jurisdictional rules.

At one point I had suggested that we bring in a person who knew the industry and knew the labor movement and have him hear what Doug McCarron's problems and disagreements were. That person was John Dunlop, a former secretary of labor. John was a Harvard economist who had been working on construction labor relations since World War II. He did not know McCarron well. Right from the start, McCarron took the position that he knew it all, but John started giving him some of his personal background. "I was the one that handed down the decision on the pile drivers in Michigan." And McCarron's eyes opened up. He could be impressed with somebody who knew what he was talking about, especially when it was something that McCarron too was very interested in. So I knew that we had picked the right guy to mediate. But once McCarron makes a decision, he likes to stick to it. He already had his mind made up. He was eager to show his independence and to get out of the AFL-CIO and the Building and Construction Trades Department – which also meant that the Carpenters would not be a part of local building trades councils, central labor councils, or state federations.

I was, of course, extremely disappointed by the outcome. I had spent my entire life working for a unified labor movement, and I knew the hardships disaffiliation had caused in the past. On a personal level, I was extremely disturbed about the problems the Carpenters' disaffiliation would cause for all of the state and local bodies that were working to build a strong labor movement in their communities. These groups enjoyed close working relationships with local Carpenters unions and with many dedicated Carpenters members who served as their officials and leaders. But the AFL-CIO is, and always will be, stronger than the sum of its parts. And as I told the Building and Construction Trades Department, our shared values would always survive disagreements among those parts.

Little did I know at the time just how quickly those values would be tested.

Preparing for the 2004 Elections. As AFL-CIO president, I did not agree with George W. Bush's course of action on Iraq. We favored a broad international coalition acting with the sanction of the United Nations. Once our troops were on the ground, we of course stood behind them. And I thought we owed them more than our prayers and our support. I thought we owed them a vision of America that was worth their sacrifice. Instead, our economy was in a ditch, and businesses were digging in deeper, laying off tens of thousands of workers, sometimes by force of circumstances, sometimes by choice. We lost something like 2.5 million manufacturing jobs that went overseas between 2002 and 2004.

That is one of the reasons the AFL-CIO supported John Kerry for president in 2004. We had a very good relationship with him throughout his years in Congress, and he had certainly been a strong supporter on legislation that was important to workers and their families.

In the early stages of the campaign, John Kerry invited me to come to his home and to sit with him at the dining room table, talking about economic policy and the main economic issues as far as workers were concerned. Some of his top advisors, who had also been advisors to President

Clinton, were there. I had Jeff Faux with me from EPI, the Economic Policy Institute, and we put together our strongest suit of issues for Kerry to focus on – issues such as the growing wage gap between workers and managers; the unemployment situation; and the need for health care reform.

Kerry was interested to learn that some large enterprises, including Wal-Mart, were making false claims about the quality of health care they provided their workers. As a matter of fact, Wal-Mart did provide health care to some management people. But what they offered workers was the opportunity to pay for their health care themselves, and the company was not providing health care for every worker who came to work in a Wal-Mart.

Political Action Through "Working America." We launched our new Working America program in the summer of 2003 with high hopes that it would help build our political organization and get us over the top in the 2004 elections. The new program did add significantly to our political base, but was not enough to put John Kerry in the White House.

Working America offered a new and potentially game-changing form of union membership. It started with the theory that union members tend to have a more progressive view of politics. We thought it likely that their nonunion neighbors, in working-class areas, might share their views, and vote accordingly, if they got the same information and the same sense of empowerment that union members got through political education and political engagement. There are millions of working people who want a voice to speak out and a chance to work to change the direction of this country. Working America offered that voice and that chance. Polls told us that millions of workers wanted to join unions, but could not, given the resistance of their employers. So we decided to reach out to them.

I thought that Karen Nussbaum was the right person to head Working America, because of her natural talents on relating to workers and the good work we had done together on organizing women. Karen knew how to send organizers out into communities to talk to people in their homes about good jobs and a just economy, and other issues like health care and retirement security. It was a good time to try this approach, because with rising health care costs and threats to pensions from company bankruptcies, such as the collapse of Enron, people were willing to speak out.

Our two Working America pilot programs, one in Cleveland and the other in Seattle, were very successful. We hired some canvassers to ring doorbells in working-class neighborhoods, trying to reach unorganized workers and see what response we could get to our political program. We found that in both cities, workers shared similar priorities whether they belonged to unions or not. And because they realized they could not do much on their own, unorganized workers wanted to become members of a larger group with similar priorities and similar interests.

They were even willing to make a modest contribution to some of the expenses of canvassing, and that was something that impressed the AFL-CIO Executive Council. I remember Jerry McEntee, for one, was not fully supportive of Working America at the outset. But he was convinced when he saw some of these polls and noted our progress. Once Jerry bought into the program as a political strategy, other unions were willing to support this new membership category which would exist alongside our regular collective bargaining membership.

The results were encouraging. In three years we built a Working America membership of one and a half million people, working-class moderates who lived in the suburbs of big cities. And that was a milestone, because there had been tremendous resistance for thirty years to creating an associate membership directly affiliated with the AFL-CIO. Once Karen figured out the right way to get past that and build a model that was successful, Working America gained a lot of support from our affiliates. It was a great opportunity to give working Americans – union and nonunion – a stronger voice.

Still, that voice was not yet strong enough to put us over the top in John Kerry's campaign. People often play Monday morning quarterback after an election, but I really felt that we supported Kerry and worked as hard as we could. We brought 750,000 members from outside the labor movement into Working America by the time of the election, and coordinated more than 225,000 union activist volunteers for voter education and outreach in Labor 2004. Even with all of that, we did not get the political change we were after. The Bush administration was running full tilt towards its goal of privatizing government services – including Social Security, Medicare, and Medicaid – deregulating business and industry, and attacking unions. One reason why George W. Bush prevailed in 2004 was his appeal to the public's fear of another terrorist attack. But another reason, more significant to us, was that we still did not have enough members. Despite all of our outreach and new programs, our numbers were still going down. We were doing some great things in organizing, bargaining, legislation, and international affairs, but it just wasn't enough.

The Debate over Union Jurisdictions. As we considered how to organize more effectively, one of the ideas under discussion was the issue of core jurisdiction. Were mixed, general unions the best structure for a labor organization? Or did it make more strategic sense for unions to concentrate in a specific sector – for manufacturing unions to concentrate on organizing manufacturing workers, and health care unions to concentrate on health care workers? Some unions thought that because they had more experience organizing a particular group of workers, they should have sole jurisdiction for those workers. Others thought that if they were having success with a variety of workers, why should they step aside? It was a sensitive topic. The UAW organizes graduate students, for example; AFSCME and the SEIU often organize the same types of public employees; and in the building trades a variety of unions go after the same types of semi-skilled workers. So one union's "core" is another's opportunity to grow.

It was a tough topic to discuss, but I wanted to share with all of our leadership what the organizing realities were for different affiliates. The discussion had to take place within the comfort level that affiliates would allow. I was not looking for the AFL-CIO to make direct recommendations to affiliates about these jurisdictional matters, but I wanted to have a discussion about potential growth and a more effective way to represent the diversity of workers. I wanted to give the affiliates' organizing directors an opportunity for informal input into the discussion.

Some people at SEIU took the discussion to mean an endorsement of the one-union-per-industry plan that SEIU's organizer, Stephen Lerner, used in a study he called "Unite to Win." That plan concentrated on union density and market share. According to Lerner, there were around 15 industrial sectors – government, mining, health care, construction, and so forth – so we only needed around 15 industrial unions. When each of those unions concentrated on increasing density in its basic markets, then we would finally have the right structure to organize for change and to take on mega-corporations like Wal-Mart and solve problems like the lack of affordable health care. How we were going to get from here to there, the study did not say.

New Unity Partnership. Then in 2003, the leadership of SEIU, the Hotel Employees, UNITE (the needletrades union), the Teamsters, the Laborers, and the Carpenters came together in a coalition called the New Unity Partnership. They were getting a lot of press and they were dropping hints that maybe I was ready to retire. But they were not openly talking about getting out of the AFL-CIO, though Doug McCarron's Carpenters had already left. They were talking about a plan to help the labor movement grow faster…and part of that plan was to force smaller unions to merge.

Of all the things the NUP was recommending, forced mergers prompted the strongest response. The reaction was, "If they think they're going to try to force me to merge, they've got another thought coming." I always liked what my assistant Denise Mitchell had to say about that: Anyone who says you can crack a whip or knock heads to force unions to change is crazy. Ed Sullivan, the president of the Building and Construction Trades Department, which included some of the labor movement's most highly skilled workers, was not having any of it. As he put it, his members neither needed nor wanted advice from "self-appointed labor 'gurus' who couldn't tell a spud wrench from a paintbrush."

On some levels, I agreed with the New Unity Partnership. I certainly could see that the status quo on jurisdictions was not getting us to our organizing goals. In fact, even before the NUP was formally organized, I had listened to their complaints and moved to set up an executive committee led by the presidents of the largest affiliates. So yes, we had to embrace change. But it had to be thoughtful change, change that was mindful of what makes a movement and respects our members and our organizations, it had to be change that made us stronger, not weaker.

SEIU's president, Andy Stern, was the most outspoken member of the New Unity Partnership. Andy took the view – one that was quite incorrect in my estimation – that the AFL-CIO under my leadership was against moving quickly enough to meet its organizing and political challenges.

Andy and I had had a very good relationship at SEIU, and I thought that Andy made a good president of the union. But when I first took over as AFL-CIO president, I had supported Dick Cordtz, the current secretary-treasurer of SEIU, over Andy to serve out my unexpired term at SEIU. No doubt that contributed to my problems with Andy down the road. Whatever the case, I was extremely disappointed at SEIU's convention in June 2004 when Andy threatened to "build something stronger" if the AFL-CIO did not make the changes he thought were necessary. The fact that he said this to all the delegates, in my presence, was an indication of how strongly he felt. And the fact that I wanted to be sitting there was an indication that I was as strong in my views as he was in his.

I felt, though, that it was not helpful for Andy to make these threats in the midst of the 2004 national election campaign. So in August, I told the AFL-CIO Executive Council that following the election, the AFL-CIO would begin a process of "evaluating where we are as a labor movement, the challenges we face, and how we need to respond for America's workers and their families." Andy and the NUP agreed to hold their peace until the elections were over.

Looking back, I now realize that Andy's was not a sudden defection, but that he had been working toward a break with the AFL-CIO for years. It remains a shame that he chose to use his considerable talents to divide the labor movement at a critical time rather than to build a stronger AFL-CIO for the benefit of all workers.

Inviting Broad Participation in the Discussion. I was hoping the unity we demonstrated throughout the 2004 campaign would help us ward off legislative attacks and energize organizing efforts. But post-election, what I called "public cannibalizing" picked up again within our movement. I found it increasingly disturbing, and not only because I was the one who was being barbecued. As anyone on the Executive Council knew, I was not one to aid my critics by throwing myself on the grill.

Instead I invited affiliates, central and state labor bodies, allied constituent groups, and others to participate in a debate over the future course of our movement and the glue that holds us together. I asked them to identify issues they felt should be addressed and make proposals for meeting our challenges and fostering union growth. But I also asked them to keep some basic principles in mind, including respect for the democratic rights of union members, the need to invest in our future, and the vital importance of unity in the face of increasingly virulent attacks on working people and unions.

We got a remarkable response: twenty-three extensive proposals came in from national unions, forty from state federations and central labor councils, three from AFL-CIO trade departments, five from constituency groups, two from Executive Council committees, two from community partner organizations, and twenty from academics and other individuals. Some were more creative than others, some more practical than others. But most of them contained clear calls to concentrate our energies and resources on new approaches to organizing and politics.

I especially appreciated the analysis offered by Bill Lucy, the president of the Coalition of Black Trade Unionists. "I do not believe that labor's problem revolves around structure," Lucy said. "I believe that to the extent that we do have a problem, it is around mission." He added, "While the size of the Executive Council may be large, it reflects who we want to organize, mobilize, and politicize."

The SEIU got its reform proposal in early. In fact, right after the election Andy sent a document called "United We Win" to the affiliates, to central bodies, and to state feds, that outlined his vision for change, including AFL-CIO authorized mergers and coordinated bargaining, a fifty percent rebate of AFL-CIO per capita taxes to be used for organizing, and AFL-CIO enforcement of an affiliate's bargaining standards and organizing budget allocations. He also set up a blog and website to get the public discussion going. And so did we.

My Point of View. There were those on the Executive Council who thought I should have taken a stronger stand against Andy and cut off his mergers-or-else talk, but that had never been my way. Instead, in small working groups, meetings of the executive committee I had established, and Executive Council meetings, we tried to figure out what would and would not work. I did not hide the fact that while I shared my critics' frustrations and most of their goals, I had no enthusiasm for reshaping the labor movement from the top down, forcing mergers and dictating bargaining standards. Frankly, I did not think a majority of affiliates would stand for it, so forcing the issue would only divide and weaken the AFL-CIO. And I really did not see how rebating per capita taxes back to the affiliates, and therefore cutting our budget in half, would in any way strengthen the Federation.

As far as I was concerned, the real questions to debate were: What kind of labor movement did we want to be? Should we run the AFL-CIO and its unions like a corporation and hand down orders from above? Or should we uphold the grassroots traditions from which the labor movement grew? It seemed to me that what we needed to do was rebuild union members' loyalty and activism then double our spending on politics and legislation so we could strengthen our fight against immediate problems – like the Bush administration's efforts to privatize Social Security – and strengthen our ongoing effort to elect friendlier officials. If we used those funds to mobilize more members for legislative and political action throughout the year, rather than concentrate on get-out-the-vote campaigns and contributions to candidates and then leverage that political action for organizing, we would be in a stronger position to help protect working families.

I thought then, as I think now, that unless we change the anti-worker policies that are destroying good jobs and stop the forces – from the National Labor Relations Board to state governments – that are rolling back workers' rights, we cannot win gains for workers.

At the AFL-CIO's March 2005 Executive Council meeting, a majority agreed with me.

New "Change to Win" Coalition Splits from the AFL-CIO. Although no final decisions would be made until the AFL-CIO met in convention in July 2005, I felt that we were making progress in our effort to decide how to use the AFL-CIO's budget for effective organizing and political work. But the vote at that March Executive Council meeting proved to be a turning point in the AFL-CIO's internal fight. As Andy Stern told the press, he did not have much faith in elected officials, whatever their party. And he certainly made it clear that he did not have much faith in the AFL-CIO either, because right after that meeting, Andy, James Hoffa of the Teamsters, Bruce Raynor of UNITE, John Wilhelm of HERE, and Joe Hansen of the United Food and Commercial Workers publicly pledged to form an alliance and merge their various reform proposals into a single set.

They made good on that pledge a few months later, in June 2005, when SEIU, the Teamsters, the Laborers, UNITE HERE (which had merged in 2004), and the UFCW formed an independent coalition called Change to Win. The following month, on the eve of the AFL-CIO convention, four Change to Win unions – SEIU, the Teamsters, the UFCW, and UNITE HERE – announced that they would boycott the meeting. They did come to Chicago where the convention was held; they registered as delegates; but they did not participate in any way. In fact, by the time the proceedings got underway, SEIU and the Teamsters had left the Federation, and later that week, the UFCW was gone too.

When I got up to address the delegates at the AFL-CIO convention I simply had no choice but to strongly criticize the unnecessary breakup of the Federation. I believed the split would weaken labor's political influence for years to come and would damage our efforts to expand union representation for working people. This split, I told the delegates, was "a grievous insult to all the unions" and a "tragedy for working people, because at a time when our corporate and conservative adversaries have created the most powerful anti-worker political machine in the history of our country, a divided movement hurts the hopes of working families for a better life."

I also argued then – and I still believe it now – that a labor movement that is divided and fighting itself weakens our ability to make electoral gains. By law the AFL-CIO can only mobilize voters who are in our member unions, so we would no longer be able to coordinate get-out-the-vote drives involving members of the disaffiliated unions. I said that division in the ranks would only feed the greedy appetites of those wanting to further turn back the clock on the gains for working men and women which took so many years to accomplish. In the arena of collective bargaining, the split only helped weaken our ability to stand together and fight those who were fighting us. In the end, workers lost and our enemies came out with a stronger hand against our interests.

So here we were, with workers under the biggest assault in eighty years. Now more than ever we needed a united labor movement. But instead of exercising our greatest strength – solidarity – to grow the movement and build real worker power, Change to Win (which also included the Carpenters by now) was creating a real divide that served the corporations and the anti-worker politicians. I was pretty sure that champagne corks were popping at the Bush White House, at Wal-Mart corporate headquarters, and on Wall Street, because it was not long before UNITE HERE, the Farm Workers, and the Laborers also left the Federation for Change to Win. As a consequence, AFL-CIO membership dropped by forty-eight percent causing the income we received from per capita taxes paid by our affiliates to drop from $91 million to $48 million and around one hundred of our staff members had to be let go. The AFL-CIO now represented forty-three percent of organized labor, down from eighty-two percent – not a very satisfying way to celebrate the Federation's 50th anniversary.

The decision to disaffiliate more than disappointed me. I thought it was one of the most destructive acts I ever witnessed. I resented it personally because I knew the issues so well and really understood what was doable and what was not, I guess that is the difference between Andy and me. I am happy to work hard on achieving something that is doable. I am not interested in going up against a stone wall on an issue such as forced mergers. Should there be mergers? Should mergers be encouraged? Of course, but do not walk all over the leadership of good local unions and tell them that they have to merge. I do not see that as a great program for any federation of equals.

Our Attempts to Find a Middle Ground. I could not really understand why the Change to Win leaders did not try harder to push their program within the AFL-CIO; I certainly felt that they could have been influential in changing things at the AFL-CIO if they were inside. I believe that Andy found the negotiating process very frustrating. He did not see things moving the way that he thought things should be moving and I think he and the others were not really looking for solutions. Their "my way or the highway" threats only undermined our ability to reach a genuine agreement built on consensus and respect, which is the only kind of agreement that would last.

In the time leading up to the convention, we did our damnedest to try and keep the dissident unions in the Federation. We listened to their complaints, weighed our options, and tried to address their major concerns. For instance a couple of months before the split, we published "Winning for Working Families," our recommendations for uniting and strengthening the union movement. Did it give them exactly what they wanted? No, because nobody was going to go for forced mergers, rather we simply recommended voluntary mergers. We also recommended establishing Industry Coordinating Committees to build more power for workers by supporting joint bargaining and organizing activities among unions with a substantial membership in a particular industry. The first ICC, formed later that fall, brought together eleven unions in the arts, entertainment, media, and information industries. And we did offer a compromise on putting more money into organizing that, I think, was viable. It was not exactly as high as what James Hoffa would have liked, but it was significantly high;

it would have produced $500 million a year for organizing, or $2.5 billion over five years, a pretty good investment.

A few weeks before the 2005 convention, we also agreed to support a proposal which would give the Federation the power to develop and enforce contract standards. The AFL-CIO would also be able to protect unions that are part of an industry-wide organizing strategy from interference by other unions within those organizing campaigns. These were big issues for the Change to Win group. But they were not interested in compromise.

On the Sunday before the convention, I had asked Ed Hill, the president of the IBEW, to meet with James Hoffa, president of the Teamsters, to find out what his bottom line really was. It was the rebate issue. He thought the per capita taxes paid to the AFL-CIO were just too high. I was hoping that it might be helpful for Jim to talk with Ed, someone he respected, but Ed could not change Jim's mind.

Change to Win's final demand to have John Wilhelm replace Rich Trumka as candidate for secretary-treasurer – with the idea that I would step down in a year and let him succeed me – seemed to confirm that their real question was: Who's going to be in charge? If I can be blunt, this group of unions wanted to dictate who the next president of the AFL-CIO would be, despite having only about one-third of the votes. But if they thought that I would submit to their power play in order to avoid a split, they were mistaken.

Our convention proceeded as usual, and Rich Trumka, Linda Chavez-Thompson, and I were re-elected. I firmly believed that, as I said in my report to the convention, "Our job as leaders of the unions that represent 13 million hardworking men and women is to move beyond division, to make our decisions together, to move forward in solidarity and get about the business of building a better future for working families."

So we tried in many ways to address their issues. But as one SEIU staffer put it, Change to Win moved the goal posts every time the AFL-CIO got close, and that made many of us conclude that power and position, not organizational structures or issues, fueled this destructive fight.

In the Aftermath of the Breakup. When Change to Win was formed, many of its supporters compared their new federation to John L. Lewis's CIO that had shaken things up in the 1930s. The same academics and scholars who heralded my election in 1995 as a revolution now expected Change to Win to do what we had not – organize the unorganized, particularly in the private sector, overnight. But as it turned out, Change to Win faced the same problems we faced, labor laws that are stacked against organizing, employers who misclassify workers to keep them out of a bargaining unit, and all the rest. All their rhetoric about organizing whole industries remained just that – rhetoric. As they told us many times, talk is cheap.

I have to say, I saw a lot of ego at play, or maybe I should say arrogance, where the leaders of Change to Win were concerned. But I think the experience may have taught a valuable lesson: Leaders cannot force their ideas but need to work very hard to develop consensus. And that is something labor leaders have had to contend with since the days of Samuel Gompers. There was a press conference on immigration a year or so after the split, and James Hoffa was asked if he was speaking for Change to Win. He looked at the reporter and he said, "No, I'm not here to talk about the Change to Win position, because Change to Win has eight different positions," meaning that the president of each affiliate had a different twist on immigration reform. It was a facetious comment, but it was also serious, because it actually represented the Andy Stern experience with Change to Win. People liked him and they respected his views, but they did not want to be forced.

From that terrible experience of the split in the AFL-CIO, I have been able to draw some positives. When I talk to young people advancing into union leadership, I do my best to tell them how important it is to hear the concerns of their own members, to engage with ordinary rank and file members, to reach consensus on disagreements within the union's ranks, and not to let personal ambition take over.

It is now over ten years since Andy Stern helped to lead the Change to Win group out of the Federation.[5] I am glad that many of the unions that left have returned into the fold of the AFL-CIO. As my predecessor Lane Kirkland said, "Sinners belong in the church." I regret that my union, SEIU, is one that has not yet returned. But I hope I will see that happen one day.

7

GRASSROOTS SOLIDARITY: HISTORIC
ELECTORAL WINS IN 2008

I was angry and I was disappointed by the schism created by Change to Win, but I was still the president of the AFL-CIO and it was my responsibility to hold the American labor movement together. Making things work for working people was what mattered to me when I first joined the labor movement, and that still mattered to me now.

I admit that my first inclination after the split was to strictly enforce longstanding rules that would keep disaffiliated local unions out of local and state labor councils. After all, Change to Win could not have it both ways. We knew the councils would suffer from the loss of those member unions, and we were taking steps to provide additional resources where the need was most acute. But we were not going to go along with the disaffiliated unions' approach to "partnerships" that basically meant that they could pick and choose which parts of the Federation they wanted to join. Frankly, we were not planning to become an "open shop" operation.

The reality was that many local unions on either side of the divide resented the split and the tensions that resulted, because local and state councils needed all those unions to work effectively. Their dissatisfaction was a testament, I think, to the value of our Union Cities program and the grassroots activities it was supporting. A lot of important work gets done on the local level, especially important political work, like coordinating mass phone-banking, canvassing, and get-out-the-vote operations. So we had to recognize this. We really were sensitive to what we and the affiliates were hearing from their local unions. And, of course, we relied on the central labor councils and the state federations for their assessment of the situation and what they thought we could do to relieve some of the tension and preserve the solidarity that existed at the local level.

Mending the Split at the Grassroots Level. So in August 2005, soon after the AFL-CIO convention and Change to Win's split with the AFL-CIO, we proposed Solidarity Charters and we got negotiations underway with the Change to Win unions. By November 2005, we had a plan to allow their local unions to rejoin the councils with full voting rights and leadership participation. The response was very positive. Around 80 percent of Change to Win locals took up the offer, so the labor movement was able to remain strong and united on the local level. Some locals that were not even affiliated with either federation took advantage of the Solidarity program to join local councils.

This was not a rash decision. The Solidarity Charters came about as a result of talking to our national affiliates first. We had a committee, Ed McElroy from the Teachers union was involved as was Tom Buffenbarger from the Machinists. We had meetings with Change to Win to discuss what we were exploring and to get their support, which we eventually received. We tried to look at it from the point of view of both AFL-CIO affiliates and Change to Win affiliates, and we had significant discussions at the local level. Mike Cavanaugh, whom we had hired away from UNITE HERE some time earlier, had a big hand in the success of the Solidarity Charter program.

We were also able to work together with Change to Win on politics. In fact just about a year after Change to Win's formation, their chairperson, SEIU Secretary-Treasurer Anna Burger, and I announced the creation of a National Labor Coordinating Committee. The committee was headed by Jerry McEntee, our long-time political committee chairman, and Edgar Romney, secretary-treasurer of Change to Win and executive vice president of UNITE HERE. Through that committee, the entire labor movement would be working together in the 2006 elections to make working people's issues a top priority. And we made a tremendous effort: A total of 205,000 members from AFL-CIO unions, Change to Win unions, and our community affiliate, Working America, volunteered their time. They visited 8.25 million homes, distributed 14 million flyers, and made 30 million phone calls. This time the election results were good: with a Democratic majority in the Senate and the House, and Nancy Pelosi as speaker, we had hope for real change.

But if we had any hope at all of passing the labor law reforms that we needed in order to grow, we still needed to elect a Democratic president and a few more Democratic senators. And that, at least, was a goal that both the AFL-CIO and Change to Win could work together to achieve.

Revving Up for the 2008 Campaign. The votes in 2006 were barely counted before we started revving up for the 2008 presidential campaign. John Edwards announced he was running before the year was out; Hillary Clinton followed in January 2007; then came Barack Obama. All told there were eight Democratic candidates to consider, and almost all of them had good labor records. So the Democrats were fielding a pretty good team.

But we did have a problem, even before primary season got underway, because of the Democrats' choice of Denver as the 2008 convention city and the Pepsi Center, a nonunion venue, as the meeting place. Colorado did not have the best labor record in its state legislature or in the governor's office. Governor Bill Ritter, a Democrat elected with our support, had struck down a bill that would have made it easier for workers to form unions. There were also very, very few union hotels in Denver, which was a big problem for us. We intended to try and get the convention moved unless we could be assured that Colorado's officials really supported our values and priorities. We sought the support of the mayor, John Hickenlooper, and I had discussions with Governor Ritter. The Teamsters made it pretty clear that they were ready to picket the convention if it came to that, and the stage hands were, understandably, balking at the prospect of having to sign a no-strike pledge with no promise of a union contract. I was meeting and talking with Howard Dean, the Democratic National Committee chairman, trying to work it all out. Finally, we were able to get a compromise on the Pepsi Center – it would be staffed with union labor for the duration of the convention.

As for the AFL-CIO's presidential endorsement, we intended to get behind a candidate that we thought would be capable of finding long-term solutions to the growing economic crisis. The collapse of the sub-prime mortgage industry late in 2007 would touch off the worst economic recession since the Great Depression. Economic anxiety was the number one topic among the people we canvassed through Working America, our community affiliate that now counted over two million members. But for workers and their families, the Great Recession was just the latest pothole on an economic low road that the country had been heading down for the last thirty years. So even if we solved the immediate economic crisis, we still had to deal with a system that paid the average CEO 400 times what the average worker made. Voters had rarely been so upset – and rightly so. Unless the country changed direction and focused on policies like health care, good jobs, fair trade, retirement security, and the right to form unions, the American middle class would disappear.

After meeting in March 2007, the AFL-CIO Executive Council decided that there was no point in rushing an endorsement; John Edwards, Hillary Clinton, Barack Obama, and Dennis Kucinich all had their supporters on the council. So we decided to include our members and their families in the endorsement process. In April, we launched an interactive website called "Working Families Vote 2008" that provided reams of information about the candidates and issues. It included links to candidate videos, polls and blogs, a forum for discussion of key issues in the presidential race, and an Action Center that allowed users to let presidential candidates know where they stood.

Around the same time we started a series of Working Families Town Meetings, so candidates could meet with union members and their families. The candidates had a unique opportunity to listen to the real concerns of working people, firsthand. And the families had a chance to ask the candidates what they intended to do to make America work for them. Questions from the floor – to Senator Obama at a meeting in Trenton, Senator Clinton in Detroit, Representative Kucinich in Columbus, Governor Bill Richardson in Phoenix, Senator Thomas Dodd in Sacramento, and Senator Joe Biden in Miami – made it clear that America's working families were looking for a national about-face on jobs and wages, affordable health care for their families, retirement security, and a firm plan for getting out of Iraq.

We topped off the town hall meetings that summer with a multi-candidate forum in Chicago. The plan was to give our members and their families a chance to listen to the candidates and to have the candidates listen to us. And we meant all the candidates – the AFL-CIO invited all Democratic and GOP 2008 contenders. No Republicans accepted the offer. The only one of the eight Democrats who declined to participate was Mike Gravel, a former senator from Alaska and a long shot at best. Originally we planned to hold the forum at McCormick Place, but the demand for tickets was so great – 12,000 requests came in – that we moved the proceedings to Soldier

Field. Keith Olbermann from MSNBC was the moderator, and MSNBC and XM Satellite Radio broadcast the event live. Union members could ask their questions from the floor, and we hosted an "Ask the Candidate" contest on our website that generated more than 1,600 questions. In the stadium and online, the crowd came out because we were so ready to change the direction of the country and we truly believed that one of the Democrats on the stage would be our next president.

There were some pretty moving questions. One of the best came from a Steelworker who had spent 34 years at LTV Steel but was forced to retire due to a disability. Then the company filed for bankruptcy two years later, and that was the end of his pension. "Every day of my life I sit at the kitchen table across from the woman who devoted 36 years of her life to my family, and I can't afford to pay for her health care," he said. "What's wrong with America and what will you do to change it?" No one was able to give a good answer. But all of them had something to say against NAFTA and something in favor of health care and the right to organize. And they were all ready to attack each other in order to prove who had the best labor credentials. So it turned out to be one of the most spirited debates of the entire campaign.

But it did not really resolve anything as far as an AFL-CIO endorsement went. The rules required a two-thirds majority vote of the Executive Council, and no candidate could claim that yet. They were all credible candidates, even Dennis Kucinich, who probably came in on the lower end of any poll. But it did make things a little sensitive for me, because they were all good friends of the labor movement and they had all done a lot to earn our support. It was not just their endorsement of the Employee Free Choice Act, proposed legislation that could remove significant barriers to union organizing. In most of their cases, it was our years of working together. I do not think it was a surprise to anybody when the field was narrowed down to two, Hillary and Barack, but it was a tough decision for a lot of people.

The Decision to Endorse Obama. Barack Obama gained significant momentum in January 2008 when Caroline Kennedy wrote an op-ed for the Sunday *New York Times* supporting his campaign. She saw him as someone who could inspire the nation to do better, just as her father, John Kennedy, had done. That same day I got a call from her Uncle Ted. I had just finished reading the paper and my wife was pushing me to get ready for church, and the phone rang and it was Teddy. I said, "I just finished Caroline's op-ed piece." He said, "Well, that's part of what I want to talk to you about. I want to give you a heads up that we have decided to endorse Obama. I'm doing a speech at American University tomorrow and I will announce it there."

I said, "Well, I'm not surprised by your decision, but I didn't expect you to make it just yet."

He told me, "We decided that we really had to get out front on it, and I think this election is going to be a tough election." He put it on a personal basis. He was very frank about how difficult John McCain could be, especially on issues like immigration. "He's a nice man," Ted said, "but he's hard to work with." And he was not shy about saying that he thought Hillary would be a great president. But he thought that Barack Obama probably had a better chance of getting elected. He thought that Obama had done a good job in his short time in the Senate, and to elect the first African American as president, I think, was something that he was very much attuned to. "Anyhow," he said, "I think that Obama would be great and we want to give him as much help as we can."

It was not the first time that Ted Kennedy had called me to give me a heads up on something that he was going to do. In the past it was mostly on legislation. I think he appreciated my reaction and my frankness, and I do not think he expected to get any opposition from me. He certainly didn't that Sunday. But at that point, the AFL-CIO still was not ready to make an endorsement.

Change to Win was. A couple of weeks after Barack Obama won most of the Super Tuesday primaries, they made their decision because, as their chair Anna Burger told the press, they thought that it was time to bring this nomination process to a close. I thought it was interesting that the Change to Win unions, especially SEIU, were spending a lot of time and money on the primaries, since the AFL-CIO's political spending was such a point of contention when they left the AFL-CIO.

We would also spend a lot of money, but we were saving it for the presidential campaign that fall. In the meantime, we were still holding meetings with Hillary Clinton and Barack Obama. Arlene Holt Baker (who had taken over as executive vice president when Linda Chavez-Thompson retired) and Rich Trumka were instrumental in developing an outreach campaign to spread the word about John McCain's economic record and disastrous health care proposals. In May we launched a grassroots campaign called "McCain Revealed." It was a massive door-to-door canvass of 200,000 union swing voters in twenty-two battleground states to educate voters on McCain's economic positions and urge McCain to shift course. We thought it was time for the senator to tune out the insurance industry lobbyists who were shaping his campaign and start listening to the real concerns of working people.

We did endorse Barack Obama once the primaries were over and Hillary Clinton was out of the race. Overall, it had been a tough contest because Hillary had some very strong supporters on the Executive Council, like AFSCME. Of course, the Hillary campaign was very upset that she did not get our endorsement early on, and that was understandable. No one doubted her experience or her commitment to our issues. But she did not get the two-thirds majority support that she needed from the Executive Council.

Rich Trumka, Arlene Holt Baker, and I with President
Barack Obama in 2009. The AFL-CIO endorsed him
and played a prominent role in his election.

By the time we invited Obama to meet with the Executive Council late in June, the fight was behind us. In fact, the meeting was like a victory party. Everybody was upbeat, everybody thought he was a sure winner, and everybody believed in him, as far as I know. I, myself, would say often, once we were moving towards the endorsement, "This is a person whom I believe in, whom I trust. I think that he means what he's saying and I think that he's going to do his damnedest." Whether it was on health care or the Employee Free Choice Act or trade policy, Barack Obama said the right things, and I think he meant them. Little did we know, little did he know, how tough it was going to be to accomplish our goals.

We were justified in our endorsement, since a significant number of affiliates and their members clearly favored Obama. And fortunately, the Clinton supporters joined in very actively in the campaign. Jerry McEntee, of course, as the president of AFCSME and our political chair, came on board, and did the same good job that he always did. Other strong leadership voices for Hillary, Tom Buffenbarger of the Machinists and Mike Sullivan of the Sheet Metal Workers, also came on board.

Getting to Know the Obamas. Now we were unified and we were proud to stand with Barack Obama to help our nation chart a course to improve life for working people and their children. As our endorsement stated, "he's a champion for working families who knows what it's going to take to create an economy that works for everyone, not just Big Oil, Big Pharma, the insurance companies, the giant mortgage lenders, speculators, and the very wealthy." He had a 98 percent voting record on working families' issues, compared to just 16 percent for his opponent, John McCain.

At that point, I did not know Obama well, but I learned all I could about him and his background, and I relied on people I knew, like the folks in Illinois, who knew him well and who were so solid for him. I wanted our members to get to know him, too, because we could not overlook the fact that there were always people who would not vote for a black person no matter what. That being the case, we made a real effort to let them know that there were hundreds of good reasons to vote for Barack Obama and one bad reason to vote against him. We had a "Meet Barack Obama" website and the AFL-CIO also put out a mailing that unions could send to their members that debunked some of the ridiculous misinformation that was out there, like Obama is Muslim, he was born in Kenya, and he would not pledge allegiance to the flag.

At one point when I was out in the Midwest working for the campaign, I got a chance to meet Michelle Obama. We were both invited to a COPE fundraiser on a Saturday night. So we were sitting together and started conversing about the family, about her husband, herself, and so on. As our conversation continued, I developed the same feeling about her as I had about him as a genuine, no-nonsense person.

I asked her, "When are you going home?"

She said, "Well, I'm going tonight. At least I want to go tonight." She added, "Barack has been working so hard, and tonight's the first night that he will have been home in a while." She was talking along the same lines that my wife and I might talk, mentioning their habit of going to church on Sunday, and then taking the girls to dance lessons, or whatever they did after church. I related to everything she was saying, the family routine, and the two little children.

So I said to her, "I'm on the program to speak before you do. You've got to speak first."

She said, "But I want to stay. I want to hear your speech."

I said, "You don't have to hear my speech. You've heard it. You get yourself on that plane. Otherwise, Barack will beat me up." She took it all in great fun.

When she got up there she told some funny stories about her husband and how hard he was working. "You know, I get worried about him. He came home the other night all bubbling over and he's obviously had a good time with the event. He said, 'Honey, you know what they were saying about me?' I said, 'No, and I don't want to hear it. Listen, Barack, baby, you're letting this stuff go to your head. You've got to come down to earth.'" It was so natural, the kind of thing that my wife would say to me if I was getting carried away. I think that they are an easy couple to know and to understand and to really like.

Solidarity in Obama's Election Victory. Whatever our differences with Change to Win, we did manage to work together to elect Barack Obama president. Fortunately, we recognized the fact that we are better together in politics than we are separate. That success probably had a lot to do with the Solidarity Charters that brought us closer together at the local level where it counted. So when we announced that we were going to work together, there was none of the second-guessing that we had seen on other issues, where some of the Change to Win affiliates wanted to work with us, but Andy for whatever reason did not. In the case of the 2008 election, there was such a desire to win and to strengthen our forces by working together. Except for minor problems along the way, our cooperation worked very well. We had all experienced the same hardships and anti-worker attitudes in the Bush administration, and we were all committed to electing Senator Barack Obama president of the United States.

On election night I felt great. We had done what we set out to do; we helped elect a Democratic president and a Democratic majority in Congress. It was really a very happy victory. Election Day 2008 was one of the brightest days in my lifetime of fighting for working men and women.

We knew the election was just step one in delivering the change we wanted. We still needed to be politically stronger to get the legislation we needed. But our assessment of Barack the person, Barack the leader, and Barack the president gave us a lot of hope. After eight years of an anti-worker administration and some awful trade policies that drastically affected manufacturing industries, we now had a president-elect who was committed to helping us reclaim our country from those who had served corporate interests and the privileged at the expense of everyone else.

So we were very happy to have a new neighbor at 1600 Pennsylvania Avenue. This time I was delighted to make that customary call to congratulate our new president.

8

THE PEOPLE'S WORK IS NEVER DONE: PREPARING TO STEP DOWN

The last lines of my 1996 book, *America Needs a Raise*, quote the Irish poet Seamus Heaney, "Once in a lifetime, the longed-for tidal wave of justice can rise up – and hope and history rhyme."

We felt we were riding that wave in the weeks and months following our political victory in 2008. With an ally in the White House and a Democratic Congress, I felt confident that we were about to cross over to a new era for America's working families, one in which workers would begin to receive a fairer share of the wealth they create and corporations and CEOs would be forced to put people before profits.

With President Obama's election, I was not the only one who thought that this was our moment to push forward health care reform, immigration reform, and labor law reform. Our corporate opponents certainly feared our potential influence on future policy-making and they were doing their best to undermine our credibility with the public.

I suppose you could say that their fears were justified, because after working our butts off to elect Obama, we did expect more than the usual consultation to select a new Labor Secretary. I was determined to do everything I could to take advantage of this longed-for tidal wave of opportunity to gain a stronger voice for working Americans in all the decisions that were made – not just on labor business but on the people's business.

The Excitement of Obama's First 100 Days. No one was taking anything for granted, but we were delighted to have a president who believed in building worker power and had no problem working with us on most issues. President Obama was consulting with us on a regular basis and he was making some spectacular appointments. Hilda Solis, our new Secretary of Labor, had marched with us, picketed with us, and as a representative from East Los Angeles, had one of the best voting records of anyone in the United States Congress. I was not surprised that she had to endure one of the toughest confirmation battles in the history of the United States Senate. Corporate-controlled members of Congress knew who she was – a warrior who stood for working people over special interests. She called herself "the new sheriff in town" and promised to turn what I had called the second Commerce Department during the Bush administration back into the Labor Department.

Other appointments also boosted our hopes. Kathleen Sebelius at the Department of Health and Human Services had a history of fighting for consumer and patients' rights. Wilma Liebman at the National Labor Relations Board had strong union ties. And Randy Babbitt at the Federal Aviation Administration was the former president of the Air Line Pilots Association and a former AFL-CIO vice president, too.

We were also pleased that during his first one hundred days in office, President Obama overturned anti-union executive orders put in place by the Bush administration, including the ban on utilizing project labor agreements on federal construction sites. He signed legislation that restored the rights of women workers to sue over pay discrimination, extended health care coverage to four million more children, and passed an economic recovery plan with real investments in infrastructure and green jobs. Although we did not get everything we needed in that plan, the debate helped us paint a public portrait of our crumbling bridges, highways, airports, and water treatment facilities. We also made the case for a broader understanding of "infrastructure" to include rebuilding our schools, restructuring our power grids, increasing access to the Internet, and even changing the way we keep and use medical records.

So compared to the Bush administration, it was like night and day. Barack Obama really reminded me a little of Franklin Delano Roosevelt, especially when he expressed the view that "You cannot have a strong middle class without a strong labor movement."

Disappointment on Labor Law Reform. Obama had pledged to sign the Employee Free Choice Act, making it easier for workers to form or join a union, and we thought passage could be accomplished within the president's first term. When the bill was first introduced during the Bush administration in 2003, pundits had said that we were on a fool's errand, but we had stuck with it. Now we thought we were on the verge of success: Polls showed that 73 percent of the public supported this legislation and so did the leadership in Congress. We knew we would still have a fight because if passing the Employee Free Choice Act was our number one legislative priority, defeating it was the corporate dream. People we had counted on, like Senator Arlen Specter, a long time Republican from Pennsylvania who switched to the Democrats in 2009, and Senator Blanche Lincoln, a Democrat from Arkansas (who were happy enough for our support during their election campaigns) had already defected by spring of 2009, so we were a handful of votes short of being able to stop a filibuster.

I was particularly disappointed when former Senator George McGovern, who had run for president back in 1972 with strong support from SEIU, also joined the anti-Employee Free Choice bandwagon. In fact just a few weeks before the Democratic convention in 2008, he had published an op-ed in the *Wall Street Journal* that equated card check with coercion and the mandatory payment of dues. After the op-ed appeared, I reminded McGovern that no one had stood up louder and clearer for his presidential run than SEIU's president, George Hardy. The late Howard Samuel, who once headed the AFL-CIO's Industrial Union Department, had served as director of "Labor for McGovern" back in the 1972 campaign. Now I asked his son, Bill Samuel, the AFL-CIO's legislative director, to talk with McGovern. But despite some conciliatory words to Bill, McGovern continued to speak out against the proposed labor law.

My Decision to Retire. During the weeks and months after the 2008 election, I was also making up my mind to retire. The time was right. I had always said I would retire once we had a Democratic president and a Democratic Congress in place. Frankly, the Bush years had been arduous, so I was really set to retire. It was time for a younger person, a bright, competent, articulate individual to have their chance.

Early on, I had told Rich Trumka that I was really looking forward to supporting him whenever I did decide to go, because no one has ever been more prepared to lead our labor movement. Rich had been a coal miner, a lawyer, a local union leader, and the president of the United Mine Workers, which he had taken over during an extremely difficult time in the union's history. He is also one of the most powerful and credible speakers ever in our movement. He proved that without a doubt during the Obama campaign when he confronted the race issue head-on in a forceful and persuasive way. As my partner for 14 years, Rich had done a great job managing the AFL-CIO's finances, and he had been a creative member of the AFL-CIO Executive Council. Rich had proved over and over again that he was not afraid of challenges and never backed down from a fight, qualities that made him the right guy for the tough job of leading the Federation.

I did not announce my decision to retire until the April 2009 meeting of the AFL-CIO Executive Council. But once I had made up my mind, my focus was on doing all that I could to tie up loose ends. I was especially interested in seeing what I could do to unify the labor movement. It was a personal issue with me, and I was determined to do my damnedest to bring both sides – the AFL-CIO and Change to Win – together. Especially after the presidential election, it seemed important to me to work as closely as we could with the Change to Win unions, although not everyone on the Executive Council agreed. Most council members strongly supported Solidarity Charters at the local level, but there was still constant tension. Some questioned whether Change to Win unions were really interested in working together with us.

A Unified Front on Legislative Priorities. My immediate concern was that both the AFL-CIO and Change to Win work together to pass the Employee Free Choice Act. David Bonior, a former congressman and member of the president's transition team, had made it clear that Obama wanted to deal with a unified labor movement, so I made sure that Andy Stern and Change to Win union representatives were always involved in all our meetings to discuss the Employee Free Choice Act. For the purpose of that legislation, we all worked together very well, despite being pretty far apart when it came to reunification. Beginning in January 2009, a number of AFL-CIO and Change to Win unions, along with Andy and me, had been meeting with Bonior. Bonior knew our issues pretty well, because he was also the chairman of American Rights at Work, a labor-supported organization he helped to establish in 2003 to advocate for workers and their right to form unions.

In April 2009, the group that had been meeting about shared legislative priorities – which also included AFSCME, the American Federation of Teachers, the Communications Workers, the Electrical Workers, the Laborers, SEIU, the Steelworkers, the Teamsters, UNITE HERE, the UAW, and the UFCW – came together as the National Labor Coordinating Committee, or NLCC. The National Education Association, the largest union in the country with over three million members, also participated. Although the NEA was an independent union that had never been part of the AFL-CIO, a number of local and state NEA chapters had directly affiliated with us through Solidarity Charters.

With the Executive Council's approval, the goal of the National Labor Coordinating Committee was to continue reunification discussions and coordinate activities on the major pending legislative matters, including national health care reform and passage of the Employee Free Choice Act. Overall, the NLCC represented some 16 million unionized workers, which gave us quite a voice.

Differences on Reunification. Although we worked pretty well together on legislative priorities, we still had a long way to go as far as reunification was concerned. At meetings of the National Labor Coordinating Committee, the same issues that had divided us before the split – jurisdiction, finances, organizing, governance, and the focus of AFL-CIO programs – divided us still. The specific issues were tough and so were the political and interpersonal dynamics. For instance, although David Bonior tried to maintain a neutral position, there was a feeling that he favored the Change to Win unions. There was also a feeling that Andy Stern was not really committed to moving forward. Some of the issues that Andy was still pushing, like forced mergers, were essentially off the table because even many of his own people did not support his position and had modified his proposals. In any case, it was too early to predict whether we would succeed or not.

It did not help that the newspapers got ahead of the story. The press reported that the NLCC was on the verge of replacing the AFL-CIO with a new federation that would focus strictly on politics, public policy, and legislative work and operate along the lines of the United Nations Security Council, with large unions holding permanent seats on its executive council and smaller unions taking turns. There was also talk that David Bonior was slated to head this new federation.

None of that was true, as I wrote in a memo following those news reports. "The AFL-CIO has absolutely no intention of converting itself into a mere political/lobbying operation, leaving other labor-movement-wide activities to individual unions to undertake on a cafeteria style pay-as-you-go basis," I wrote. "Nor does it view the current reunification process as one by which some newly created organization will emerge." We were interested in hearing any and all suggestions on how to improve the AFL-CIO's structure and programs, and we would certainly welcome back any Change to Win unions that wanted to come back once the process was over. But the formation of the NLCC did not mean that we were disbanding to start anew, or that we were abandoning our historic mission of fighting for economic, social, political, and workplace justice on every level.

The fact that I would be retiring at the AFL-CIO convention that fall also complicated the reunification process. I thought it was important to bring Rich Trumka in on any discussions that involved the future. And as we got closer to September 2009, when I would step down, it became apparent to me that Rich needed to be in those reunification discussions, especially if any major decisions were to be made. He could have added so much to the discussion on issues like governance and the allocation of resources. Unfortunately, some of the Change to Win unions were reluctant to have him in those discussions. It was no secret that Rich and James Hoffa had some personal differences that predated the split. That made the whole process very uncomfortable for me, and they knew exactly how I felt.

My Last AFL-CIO Convention. By the time the AFL-CIO met in convention in September 2009, we were not quite as enthusiastic about the Obama administration as we had been just a few months earlier. I still supported the president, especially on his handling of the economic crisis that he had inherited from the Bush administration, which was still dragging the country down. But I do think Rich Trumka captured our overall feeling when he gave the president an A for effort but an incomplete for results. The fact that the Employee Free Choice Act had been pushed to the back burner – the president made it very clear that he supported the legislation, but he was going to focus on health care first – was very frustrating. We were so hungry to get this legislation, since it promised to be a far-reaching step in the organizing process and in terms of updating the National Labor Relations Act. I even supported modifying the card check provision if that would get us closer to the finish line.

In my last official report as AFL-CIO president, I was more concerned with looking forward than looking back. I was optimistic about our future, because as I said then, we were living in "a special moment in history, one in which the things we want for workers and their families are very possible." While I acknowledged that the tasks before us remained daunting, I said, "If there is one thing we've learned over the past 14 years, it is this: Miracles present themselves on the shoulders of commitment, unity, and action."

At the 2009 AFL-CIO Convention I was proud to pass the "baton" on to the new AFL-CIO President and my good friend, Rich Trumka.

I was satisfied that I had given the AFL-CIO my best shot. Working from the top down and the bottom up, we had built the strongest grassroots political operation in our country; we had connected with millions of non-union workers through our community affiliate, Working America; and we had developed a partnership with the National Day Laborers' Organizing Network, which serves low-wage immigrant workers who often face the harshest forms of workplace exploitation. I was proud that many programs we had started during my presidency were still going strong. The fact that union density had increased for the first time in 50 years in 2007 and 2008 was also satisfying, and so was the increasing diversity of our members and leaders as evidenced on our convention floor. If I was disappointed that our efforts to reunify the labor movement had not worked out, it was a great pleasure to witness the re-affiliation of UNITE HERE by the time our convention ended and to learn that the Laborers were also talking about coming back.

The convention itself was very gratifying. My family, the most caring and supportive family anyone could hope for, was there – my wife Maureen, my son John, my daughter Trish, and her daughter Kennedy, along with my sisters Cathy and Peggy, my brother Jim, and a fair number of in-laws and offspring. There were kind words; everyone from Rich Trumka to Caroline Kennedy to President Obama had good things to say. There was also a video tribute that really touched my heart, it covered my career from the early days with the ILGWU and all the strikes, community meetings, rallies, organizing campaigns, and all the rest that shaped my development as a leader.

When Trish and Kennedy took the stage to introduce the tribute, my first thought was "What am I in for now?" After watching it I could only say "thank you" to both of my families – my relatives and my union sisters and brothers. I never had any illusion that I accomplished what I did alone, and it was a real pleasure to thank my partners Rich Trumka, Arlene Holt

Baker, and Linda Chavez-Thompson; my executive assistant Bob Welsh and my administrative assistant Liz Maiorany, who had worked with me for 30 years; the members of the Executive Council who had been with me every step of the way since 1995; and the many state and local leaders who kept the movement moving. "Brothers and sisters, this week isn't about what Sweeney has done, it's about what you have done," I said, "Thanks to your commitment, your personal sacrifice, and your hard work, we've taken our Federation in a new, positive, progressive direction."

My family – Maureen, John, Trish, and little Kennedy – joined me for my final AFL-CIO convention in Pittsburgh, 2009.

No Regrets. In my life's work, I have been inspired by the motto of Iona College, "Fight the Good Fight." That is all any of us can do. The results must be left to God.

While of course there were things that I wished I could do over, I had no regrets as I left the AFL-CIO. I could say with confidence and conviction that the past 14 years had been the most rewarding of my entire life, and that now I was looking forward to seeing others do an even better job.

With all the accolades and thanks and tributes, I could not help thinking back to another time, back around 2000, when I first became president of TUAC, the Trade Union Advisory Committee to the Organisation for Economic Co-operation and Development. Bob White, the president of the Canadian Labour Congress, and I were meeting with some heads of state in Paris. Bob was born in Northern Ireland, and we enjoyed each other's friendship and enjoyed working together. I learned a lot from Bob.

As we made our way to the meeting, Bob turned around and he said, "Sweeney, did you ever think that two Irish kids would be walking together up the steps of the Grand Palais, going to see the president of France?"

My answer? "No way, Bob."

Suffice it to say, I had a very satisfying career.

9

STILL FIGHTING THE GOOD FIGHT: MY ACTIVE RETIREMENT

Growing up, my sisters used to say that I liked being in charge, and I would not be completely honest if I said I didn't miss it now that I am not in charge. But retirement has its perks. I have the chance to spend more time with my family, especially with my granddaughter Kennedy who always puts a smile on my face. When she was just a toddler at church on Sunday, she would call out "Pop Pop" whenever I came up the aisle to help take up the collection. People would laugh because they knew exactly who it was. And now Maureen and I get more opportunities to laugh together with her.

While not being sure of what the future would bring, I knew I was going to enjoy an active retirement. I was open to the possibilities of where I could still be helpful. But one thing I was not going to do was compromise myself or the labor movement in any way. I think when you leave office after being entrusted to protect the interests of your membership, you have an important legacy to uphold. I knew that whatever I did in my retirement, I would endeavor to further the interests of working men and women.

The Personal Touch in Politics. I always say I retired from my job, not my life, and I've certainly kept up my political activities. The difference is that now I'm more focused on the local races and grassroots mobilization: My wife, my daughter Trish, and I man the phone banks and ring doorbells, and I enjoy it very much because you can never underestimate the value of the personal touch when it comes to elections.

I always remember a story Tip O'Neill told about ringing doorbells. After an election his staff gave him a list of people from his neighborhood who had not voted. And he said, "I can't believe that Mrs. Riley didn't vote for me. I'm going to find out why."

On his way home, he stopped at Mrs. Riley's house, rang the doorbell, and Mrs. Riley said, "Oh, Mr. Speaker. To what do I owe the honor?"

"Well," he said, "I just learned that you didn't vote the last time, and as far as I can remember, you've voted for me for years."

She said, "Well, I didn't vote for you this past election because you didn't come and ask me."

Tip was always one who realized how important it was to make personal contact, and I am still following that advice and doing what I can do on the political front.

Overseeing Workers' Pension Capital. My retirement from the AFL-CIO also gave me time to involve myself more deeply in an issue I see as a significant part of our struggle for workplace justice, namely, the responsible stewardship of labor's pension capital. When that capital is invested responsibly, it is a powerful tool for advancing the values and interests of working men and women.

Since my days as president of SEIU, I have been active in the AFL-CIO's pioneering work of developing prudent, economically targeted investment strategies for labor's pension capital. In addition to my political volunteering, my retirement has also given me the chance to expand my role on the board of the AFL-CIO Housing Investment Trust, I became Chairman in 2009. I also became the longest serving Trustee, having sat on the Board continuously since the fund's creation in 1983. With more free time I started attending more events at construction sites where new affordable housing was being built. I have been able to travel all over the country meeting union construction workers, local government officials, and affordable housing developers.

Unexpected Honors. Retirement has brought me some unexpected honors. As AFL-CIO president I had collected more than my fair share of honorary degrees, but I was pleased when Georgetown University, the preeminent Catholic institution and Jesuit stronghold, recognized my work just as I was about to retire. Then Iona College, my alma mater, awarded me an honorary degree in 2010. As far as I am concerned, these are honors for the millions of workers I have been privileged to represent, but I would be lying if I said I wasn't pleased by the recognition.

I was particularly touched in 2014 when Rich Trumka honored me at a ceremony at the AFL-CIO and presented me with the George Meany-Lane Kirkland Lifetime Achievement Award for Global Workers' Rights. This was so unexpected and so moving to me. I was truly humbled when Rich described me as someone who has "lived his core values of fairness, faith, and family" and who has "given a voice to countless workers who deserve to be treated with dignity and fairness." As one who was inspired by my faith and by the example of the Jesuit priests at Xavier to find meaning by serving in the labor movement, I cannot imagine a more meaningful tribute.

I had a chance to revisit Ireland when Ulster University recognized my work for peace and justice in Northern Ireland, presenting me with the International Conflict Research Institute (INCORE) Global Peace and Social Justice Award. The university has also created a full scholarship in my name that is available to American students with union ties who aspire to be part of the next generation of peace builders. The John J. Sweeney Scholarship is given in conjunction with the university's John Hume and Thomas P. O'Neill Chair in Peace and is supported with donations from the AFL-CIO and the American labor community. It is such a privilege to have my name linked now and into the future with Ulster's internationally recognized peace studies program.

With the President and First Lady in the Oval Office
after receiving the Presidential Medal of Freedom in
2011, surrounded by my family members.

Probably the greatest and certainly the most unforeseen honor was receiving the Presidential Medal of Freedom in 2011. I never thought for a moment that I would be nominated because it is a very prestigious award, the nation's highest civilian honor. After I got the word, I began thinking back on the other recipients from the labor movement – George Meany, Cesar Chavez, Walter Reuther, Dolores Huerta, Monsignor George Higgins, and Lane Kirkland, among others. I remember attending the ceremony for Lane when I was still at SEIU, and it was a pretty impressive moment. Now it seemed as if things had come full circle as I accepted the award on behalf of hard-working Americans, whether organized or not. My success was really their success.

I did have to laugh, though, when I learned what some of my political opponents had to say. One headline read: "Obama Gives Medal of Freedom to Socialist Crony." Apparently I was a socialist and fellow-traveler who dedicated my life to radicalizing the labor movement and promoting Barack Obama's career. It seemed funny to me that they did not complain when Monsignor Higgins got the award in 2000. He was much more of a socialist than I am.

Going to Harvard. I never expected to find myself lecturing at Harvard – and I am sure some of the Harvard professors thought the same thing. But when Harvard's Institute of Politics offered me a resident fellowship in 2010, I was really eager to take it. The program was designed to put Harvard students, particularly undergraduates, in touch with politicians, activists, and policymakers, to get them thinking about public service and leadership. The fellows in residence with me were a pretty impressive group: There were two former mayors, one former congressman, a former high-level White House staffer, and the former Prime Minister of Haiti. For three months we would all be leading study groups, delivering lectures, and engaging students in our particular specialties. My topic was "The Future of American Unions and Politics."

It was a great opportunity to educate the next generation of leaders on the value and promise of unions and to give them a chance to interrogate me on the hows and whys of the labor movement. It was also an opportunity for me to learn as well as teach, and I was not disappointed. Right from the start I involved myself in all aspects of campus life, from sitting in on classes, to sharing pizza with groups of students, to mentoring students before and after my study group, which met at the John F.

Kennedy School of Government. Students seemed surprised that I was willing not only to show up but to participate in events sponsored by campus groups like the Progressive Caucus. But that is what I was there for. I really enjoyed the connections I made with the students. I was not pushing any agenda; I left it to them to decide what they wanted to get out of their time with me.

The study group had sessions once a week. With my subject being the future of the labor movement, I was able to lecture on topics on which I had strong views, such as the country's financial crisis, political activism, and social justice campaigns. And I was able to bring in some pretty powerful guest speakers, including Damon Silvers, the director of the AFL-CIO's Policy Department, who gave an excellent talk on economic choices and challenges; Liz Shuler, who succeeded Rich Trumka as the AFL-CIO's secretary-treasurer, who spoke very enthusiastically on motivating young workers; and AFSCME President Jerry McEntee, who rallied the students with a talk on people-centered politics. Of course, the highlight was Rich Trumka. His presentation on building a new economy to restore hope and raise working families' expectations was as dynamic as you might expect.

During my time on campus, I was very pleased to accept an invitation to speak at Harvard's Trade Union Program, which offers a six-week executive training course for trade union leaders and staff. Dr. Elaine Bernard, a labor historian, directs the program (which dates back to 1942), and her students were all active in their unions, either as organizers, running political campaigns, or serving as officers. It was a level of union leadership that I really appreciated.

These were three extraordinary months for me: mixing on campus with students and faculty; speaking at dormitory programs; addressing students in the business school. The students I met were bright and energetic, and I hope that I helped increase their understanding of why a strong labor movement is so vital to America's social and economic future.

In 2014, the 80th birthday of Local 32BJ coincided with my own 80th year. I returned to the local union that gave me my start in SEIU to join the celebration. Shown with me (from left): 32BJ President Héctor Figueroa; Mary Kay Henry, President of SEIU; and Mike Fishman, a former president of 32BJ and now Secretary-Treasurer of SEIU.

10

MY 30 YEARS WITH THE HIT: THE POWER OF PENSION CAPITAL

In 1983, Lane Kirkland, President of the AFL-CIO at the time, asked for my advice in restructuring the AFL-CIO Mortgage Investment Trust, the fund which the AFL-CIO had established nearly 20 years earlier as a union-friendly vehicle for pension investment. He was concerned that the MIT was unable to achieve the original goals set forth by the AFL-CIO: earning competitive returns for union pension funds by investing in the construction of union-built affordable housing. Lane was being advised to create a new fund, which would become the Housing Investment Trust. He also wanted to resolve the legal issues that had arisen from the formation of the MIT. Lane came to me knowing that I was a strong supporter of the program. I also sat on the MIT's Board of Trustees so I saw it as my responsibility to gin up support, as well as investment capital, for the new fund. Lane and I spoke with my friends and fellow union Presidents John Deconcini of the Bakery Workers, Frank Hanley of the Operating Engineers, and Jack Joyce of the Bricklayers, to enlist their support for the creation of the HIT. In fact, SEIU – along with the Bakery Workers, Operating Engineers, and Bricklayers – were the inaugural investors in the

HIT. We were all asked to serve on the Board of Trustees. I am proud to say that SEIU was the second largest investor when the HIT was established.

We came to our responsibilities with the resolve to make the HIT a vehicle that could produce a double bottom line results for its investors: competitive returns coupled with the important collateral benefits of affordable housing and union construction jobs. We wanted the HIT to make a difference in local communities and to encourage new relationships between the grassroots labor movement and local progressive organizations. This would require that the newly formed HIT step up its investments and do more construction lending than the MIT had done. It would also require that HIT grow its capital dramatically. It would take almost a decade to achieve this quantum leap.

The American Labor Movement and Housing. Backtracking a bit, I should explain the origins of the AFL-CIO's involvement in housing. The American Labor Movement has been involved in housing for over a hundred years. In fact, Sidney Hillman, the founder and legendary leader of the Amalgamated Clothing Workers Union, was among those who proposed the creation of the Federal Housing Agency and he worked with FDR and the Congress to make it happen. What Sidney Hillman had done financing housing for working families in New York City was not only the stuff of legends, it was the working model for the new FHA.

The game changer that allowed unions to directly finance housing creation was a set of amendments to U.S. labor law that allowed unions to negotiate with employers to create pension funds to help their members save for retirement and provide for health care coverage. In the 1950s, the amount of capital in union pension plans was minuscule, but there was an abiding belief that one day labor's capital would be a significant player in financial markets. Leadership across the labor movement took advantage of the opportunity and thousands of local pension funds were established.

The AFL-CIO sponsored local education and training programs to promote both interest and understanding of what union pension capital could become. By the 1990s, labor's capital had reached the $400 billion level. [6] It was a potential force for better behavior in capital markets.

With so many pension plans newly established, the AFL-CIO went looking for ways for unions to invest their money that would be consistent with the values of the American Labor Movement. In the 1960s, the U.S. was in turmoil over civil rights, the Vietnam War, and the Cold War. It was also a time when the AFL-CIO's first president, George Meany, was having conversations with Dr. Martin Luther King, Jr., about the mutual interests of the Civil Rights and Labor movements in social and economic justice.[7] Those discussions led to Meany's belief that labor's capital could be invested strategically to help bring about needed social change, most effectively through building good quality low-income housing and creating good family-supporting jobs.

As a result of those conversations, the AFL-CIO's General Board voted in 1964 to approve the creation of the Mortgage Investment Trust and an auxiliary housing corporation, which would provide local sponsors with technical assistance and start-up working capital. George Meany, Lane Kirkland, and the other members of the General Board envisioned an investment program that would finance the construction of housing while creating union construction jobs and earning a higher rate of return than corporate or government bonds. And the auxiliary housing corporation was to partner with non-profit sponsors to develop low-income housing that could restore inner-city neighborhoods.

As I explained earlier, the MIT was never able to live up to these lofty ideals. This is where the HIT comes in to the story. While the HIT was created in 1983, its growth in the first decade was modest. Federal regulators permitted the capital invested in the MIT to "roll over" to the HIT but the fund struggled to raise additional capital. In 1991, the SEIU was one of many major union investors that helped persuade two large public employee retirement funds to commit $100 million each to the HIT. This was the first turning point: The HIT now had $500 million of investment capital. Those of us on the HIT's Board of Trustees felt that now was the time to begin the next phase of growth. The AFL-CIO wanted the capital level to reach $1 billion by the end of the decade, and the Board wanted projects financed across the country. It was then that the Board asked Richard Ravitch, an old Labor ally and an accomplished housing developer from New York, to accept the chairmanship of the HIT's Board. Ravitch brought great knowledge to the tasks ahead and a strong belief that the HIT would reach its goals if it had the right person leading it. He also thought that the HIT could grow larger than our $1 billion goal.

Looking for a New CEO. For almost a year, the Board interviewed candidates to succeed Floyd Hyde, who had stepped in when the first CEO of the HIT, John Evans, died suddenly. Floyd, who had the distinction of making Nixon's Enemies List, had been a young Marine on Iwo Jima and had also served as the very able mayor of Fresno, California. He brought professionalism and stability to the HIT, but indicated a desire to move on to another phase in his life. In August of 1991, Lane called me and said Ravitch had found a candidate for the CEO job. It was Steve Coyle, who was then serving as Mayor Ray Flynn's Director of the Boston Redevelopment Authority. He took the job in early 1992.

Steve came to the HIT with a lot of experience in housing and community development – seven years as the Director of the BRA and three years as Executive Assistant to HUD Secretary Patricia Harris. Some of my building trades colleagues already knew Steve from his work in those two positions. Everything done by the BRA under his tenure was built union, including a number of affordable housing developments and all major downtown work. Among Steve's first steps was to appoint Mike Arnold, a dyed-in-the-wool bricklayer, and his former colleague Rod DuChemin to the job of making certain that all of HIT's projects would be wall-to-wall union. We knew this was key to getting the support we needed from the building trades to expand the HIT's investment program.

Steve also came with a lot of ideas about how to grow the fund and the HIT's business. When he took the helm, net assets doubled in four years to over $1 billion in 1995 and doubled again five years after that. Steve instituted changes to all aspects of the HIT's business which positioned the HIT to grow into the nearly $6 billion fund it is today. In the process, the HIT financed projects all over the country, creating affordable housing and union construction jobs, and began to fulfill the vision of George Meany and Dr. Martin Luther King, Jr.

Achieving Meany and King's Vision. With Ravitch and Steve Coyle, the HIT began focusing on developing relationships with Fannie Mae and state and local governments and creating initiatives to guide investments. The HIT also began working with state housing finance agencies in earnest and even worked with members of the United States Congress and HUD to create the Community Investment Corporation Demonstration Program, a federal initiative under which the HIT financed 18 projects in very low income neighborhoods in places such as El Paso, Atlanta, and Los Angeles.[8]

In addition, the HIT created a subsidiary, Building America CDE, during my first year as Chairman of the Board in 2009. I saw this organization as the "auxiliary housing corporation" that the AFL-CIO's General Board proposed in 1964. Building America is able to provide New Markets Tax Credits to aid the development of commercial and housing projects in underserved communities. This helped the HIT to create union jobs in markets where it had never been active before and expanded its reach beyond housing into commercial developments. In 2016 the HIT entered into the "401(k) world" with the creation of a new fund, the HIT Daily

Valued Fund. The HIT-DVF is able to accept capital from the growing defined contribution market and was introduced to the Board during my time as Chairman. The HIT is also working to create another fund that could provide upfront capital to get affordable housing and community development projects off the ground.

Fifty years have passed since President Meany laid out his vision in a letter to the General Board of the AFL-CIO of a fund that would use union pension capital to develop affordable housing and generate union construction jobs and could also provide for the secure retirement of union members. I believe the HIT is fulfilling that vision and will continue to do so for years to come.

From $104 million to $10 billion. I have been fortunate to be a part of the HIT's growth from $104 million when I joined the board in 1984 to nearly $6 billion today. The fund even grew during the Great Recession. I credit this success to the solid support that the HIT receives from across the union movement, especially grassroots building trades funds, and to the dedicated investment team that Steve Coyle has developed at the HIT. The HIT has also benefited greatly from the perspectives of its capable and engaged union-management board. The HIT's Board has been led for much of the past two decades by Richard Ravitch, the former New York State lieutenant governor.

Ravitch has a unique perspective and understands the interplay between labor, politics, and real estate making him and effective emissary to politicians and public officials across the country. The Board's union Trustees, which by rule always include the AFL-CIO president and the head of the Building Trades, have given just as much to the Board. Rich Trumka has continued my strong support of the HIT, and the fund's growth since he became President in 2009 has been phenomenal. And, from Bob Georgine to Sean McGarvey, the Building Trades have been staunch supporters of the HIT. Management Trustees and Union Presidents, leadership and staff, we all have worked together to grow the fund to $10 billion and beyond so that the HIT can continue to invest in communities for years to come.

Since Coyle, Ravitch, and I come from very different backgrounds, we have had occasional disputes about the timing or sequencing of programs and initiatives over the years. Even when we disagree, we have never lost sight of what we have all tried to create – a unique investment program that shows there is a better way to manage "Labor's Capital." We know we are doing the right thing when we meet union construction workers who are glad that their retirement capital is being invested in their communities creating homes and jobs or families walking into their new homes for the first time. When we see HIT's performance record, we realize that a labor-sponsored fund can beat Wall Street while investing in Main Street.

I sometimes wonder what the 1964 General Board members would say if we could somehow bring them into a room today to report on how much has been done to make the HIT into what it is today. Perhaps, simply, they would ask, "What took so long?" What has been done is a tribute to the men and women in the labor movement who gathered in 1964 and voted to create this program and those in 1983, who voted to continue it. It is also a tribute to the working men and women who build the HIT's housing projects – buildings that will be home to over one million people over their useful life. And of course it is a tribute to the union pension beneficiaries whose pension savings make the HIT's investments possible. After working together for almost twenty years, Steve Coyle, Ravitch, and I have learned to use our combined skill sets to grow the HIT and to make a difference in the lives of working people.

Labor's Commitment to the Nation. Organized labor is often criticized by our adversaries as just another "special interest." But to paraphrase George Meany, our "special interest is the American people." Never before have union members embodied this more than in the moments, days, and weeks, after the September 11 terrorist attacks. I remember how everybody, in America and across the globe, was just so shocked. Everybody wanted to do something. At first it was, how do we rescue them? Then, how do we deal with the number of people who have lost their lives? How can we help the spouses and the children? It was just so sad, and yet things had to be put into action as quickly as possible. The Firefighters in New York City were outstanding, and so were the tradesmen who rushed to the scene to help to them out, running water to the Firefighters, shoring up the site, hauling away buckets of rubble, and doing whatever they could to help Firefighters search for victims. As one of them put it, "We all had one goal that day and that was to rescue and recover as many people as possible, regardless of the danger to ourselves." The general public tends to value organized labor most in times of crisis. That is probably because we have an incredible ability to come together and work together when the going gets tough. A crisis situation really shows what we can do.

I would say that union-created funds like the HIT embody organized labor's commitment to the American people and their communities. These funds give union members a way to put their retirement money to work in a way that benefits themselves, their unions, and their communities. The HIT has invested over $10 billion of union pension capital into more than 400 union-built development projects. HIT-financed projects have brought affordable housing and union construction jobs to more than 100 neighborhoods in 29 states.

Those projects are benefiting union members, of course, but also residents of the broader community. In fact, HIT investments have acted as a $25 billion stimulus program for America's communities because of the way construction investments ripple through the economy. HIT-financed construction has helped generate over 160,000 jobs across industries, including 75,000 union construction jobs, which created close to $10 billion of personal income in our communities.

John J. Sweeney

By putting union members' retirement savings to work building communities, the HIT is helping shape a world that really exemplifies union values, a world filled with family-supporting jobs, close by afford-able housing in vibrant neighborhoods, and financial security in retire-ment. That is a world where working families can thrive.

An Ambassador of Union Values. Over my thirty years as a Trustee and Chairman, I have had the opportunity to visit many of the projects financed by the HIT, and I have seen how these projects offer living proof of what the union movement is all about. I like to think that these HIT-funded projects are ambassadors of union values.

In 1999, for example, I helped cut the ribbon reopening of the his-toric Carl Mackley Apartments in Philadelphia. These apartments had been built in the 1930s by the old Full Fashion Hosiery Workers Union, one of the forerunners of UNITE-HERE. This was one of FDR's New Deal projects, built with funds from the Public Works Administration. But now, 60 years later, the housing was outdated and run down. HIT's investment helped update the aging housing complex and keep it affordable to low-in-come families. At the ribbon-cutting – where I was joined by Philadelphia's then-mayor, Ed Rendell, and local labor leaders – I particularly enjoyed talking with the young children and their parents who were thrilled to be moving into the newly renovated units.

At about that same time, San Francisco's mayor, Willie Brown, was seeking investments to revitalize the city's South Beach neighborhood. The HIT was able to help by investing in the construction of new housing for the area, an apartment building known as One Embarcadero South. When I visited the construction site, I had a chance to meet and talk with many of the union workers who built it. They were so appreciative that their pension capital had made the project possible. At the project's dedication, Mayor Brown and the HIT signed a pledge of continued investment in affordable housing in San Francisco. That is a promise we have kept. Since then, the HIT has invested more than $200 million to support development in the city.

I was pleased to go back to my native Bronx in 2000 to help kick off the renovation of the Workmen's Circle Multi-Care Center. This is a place with a long labor history, having been founded in 1951 by Workmen's Circle, an organization with ties to the early needle trades unions. When the HIT-financed renovations and expansion were completed, the nursing facility was up to date and provided permanent jobs for 475 members of SEIU 1199 and OPEIU 153.

Sometimes it takes real ingenuity to make the financing work in a high-cost city like Boston, and fortunately the HIT has the know-how to make it happen. A good example is the Rollins Square Development in Boston's diverse South End neighborhood. Rollins Square was created in 2002 to house families at risk of being displaced when the South End became a prime target for redevelopment. The project initially faced financing difficulties, but a direct loan from the HIT allowed construction to go forward. The complex financing for that project involved more than a dozen sources of funding, a real test of the HIT's expertise! When the HIT's Executive Committee held a vote to approve the investment, it was deadlocked until I cast the tie-breaking vote. I did it for one simple reason, it was the right thing to do.

I think the HIT project that has moved me most deeply is the Elizabeth Seton Pediatric Care Center in Yonkers, not too far from where I grew up. The HIT's $100 million investment there – its largest single investment at that time – helped finance the construction of a state-of-the art pediatric care facility. This special facility serves medically fragile children, mainly from lower-income families, many of whom cannot walk, eat, or breathe independently. The lovely campus replaced cramped and aging quarters in Manhattan, and the building is specially designed to make children and their families feel like it's a home, not an institution.

Especially memorable to me is the excitement I saw in the eyes of the two young people, Stephanie and Josh, who cut the ribbon to open their new home. I was so touched by their spirit, and by the spirit of the people who care for them there so lovingly. Some of these staff people are members of 1199 SEIU United Healthcare Workers East, whose collective bargaining agreement assured that their jobs would be transferred from the old location. Not only is the pediatric center close to where I lived in Yonkers, but it is sponsored by the Sisters of Charity, the order of nuns who taught me in school there. I feel so proud that through the HIT, I had a small part in bringing this wonderful facility to life.

Responding to Critical Capital Needs. There have been times over the years when the AFL-CIO has asked the HIT to develop investment initiatives to aid communities in distress. That was certainly true in the wake of the terrorist attacks on September 11, 2001.[9] All of Labor came together that day. Union firefighters, union construction workers, union medical professionals, and union social workers contributed their talents and energy in and around Ground Zero. Members of the Marine Engineers, the Masters, Mates and Pilots, and the Seafarers were operating fireboats and evacuation ferries. Our state federations and central labor councils were coordinating food, drink, and clothing for rescue workers. Our AFL-CIO Community Services network was assisting with counseling for the families of victims, our Union Community Fund was soliciting financial and in-kind donations, and many AFL-CIO unions set up special funds and activities to help.

As part of the AFL-CIO's response to this tragedy, I announced the creation of the HIT's New York City Community Investment Initiative. The AFL-CIO Housing Investment Trust and the AFL-CIO Building Investment Trust both pledged $250 million each of workers' pension capital to help New York City rebuild. The city was in shock, and it had an urgent need for investment capital. The HIT pledged to finance housing for working families to support the city's revival. The AFL-CIO was also worked with employers to get businesses up and running again.

Within just a few months of the attacks, the first of the HIT-financed housing projects was already under construction. Hudson Crossing, broke ground in early 2002 as Manhattan's first residential construction project since the attacks on the World Trade Center. Over the next twelve years, the HIT's New York City initiative would invest close to $800 million to develop or preserve the affordability of nearly 30,000 units of housing for New York City residents. In the process, the HIT created more than 5,000 on-site union construction jobs plus nearly as many other jobs elsewhere in the city. As a native New Yorker, it meant a great deal to me to see the labor movement help the city's economy recover and move forward.

Long-term Investment Strategies for Sustained Impact. One of the HIT's defining values is its sustained commitment to cities. Just as was done with the pledge to San Francisco's mayor in 1999 and to the city of New York after 9/11, we have taken this idea of community investing to other cities. These community investment initiatives have had real success in bringing labor together with public officials and community groups to create long-term solutions to affordable housing needs. Over the years I have announced many major long-term HIT commitments to cities such as Boston, Chicago, St. Louis, Minneapolis, and Saint Paul. The HIT first invested in Boston in 1984, the first of nearly thirty projects so far. In Chicago, the Trust has invested in nearly twenty projects in the last decade. St. Louis Mayor Francis Slay recognized the $400 million plus invested in the city by presenting HIT with the 2010 Mayor's Award. In the last twenty-five years, the HIT has invested over $800 million in almost seventy projects in the Twin Cities metro. And these are just a few of the places where the HIT's long-term investment strategy has led to hundreds of developments that are making a tremendous impact in American communities.

A Union-Based Stimulus Program for the Great Recession. I am particularly proud of how the HIT responded when the nation's economy was devastated by the Great Recession. Its Construction Jobs Initiative allowed union pension capital to become a much-needed source of jobs and economic recovery. Soon after President Barack Obama took office in 2009, the White House asked the AFL-CIO what we could do to help, and the Construction Jobs Initiative became part of our response to high levels of unemployment in the construction industry.

Construction is an excellent economic stimulus. Through its Construction Jobs Initiative, the HIT would invest $2.4 billion in 96 union-built community development projects in order to jump-start the economic recovery in some 30 cities. These construction projects created over 23,000 union construction jobs in eight years, plus more than 29,000 other local jobs. Union capital invested by the HIT helped keep food on the table for these construction workers and their families, while creating badly needed affordable housing for working families. In fact, those investments created or preserved almost 30,000 housing units and generated $1.6 billion in wages and benefits for union workers. The investments' ripple effects across the economy stimulated almost $8 billion of economic activity at a time when the construction industry was practically dead.

I should point out that the Construction Jobs Initiative was a win-win for the HIT's investors. Those job-generating investments provided HIT investors with competitive returns – quite an accomplishment when markets were down and so many investment funds were in the red. The HIT's investment strategy during the recession really exemplifies the labor movement's philosophy of responsible investing. Unions can teach Wall Street a lesson or two about the value of investing on Main Street and making our assets work for us – helping to grow our communities and keep our people on the job.

Revisiting Penn South Where I Heard President Kennedy Speak. There are so many more stories like the ones I have told here, stories that show what our union movement is all about: anchoring a neighborhood revitalization effort at the site of a demolished highway in Milwaukee – bringing needed medical facilities to rural Oregon – repairing damage from the destructive Superstorm Sandy in Brooklyn – creating green jobs and energy-conserving affordable housing from Boston to San Francisco – and many, many others. I must mention one more that I feel brings my experience with union-financed housing full circle.

In 2011, a couple of years after my retirement from the AFL-CIO, my work as HIT's chairman took me back to the Penn South housing cooperative in New York City. That is where, as a young man nearly 50 years earlier, I had been inspired by the words of President John F. Kennedy when he attended the grand opening of this ILGWU-sponsored co-op. This time, I was back there to lead a celebration of the HIT's $134 million investment of workers' pension capital to renovate the aging Penn South development and to keep it affordable to working families. Kennedy's call for union action, in that clipped Boston accent, echoed in my mind and to this day I can hear his words about how important the labor movement is to ensuring that our society is more just and equitable.

As I spoke to the current Penn South residents, the local labor leaders, and the New York City officials in attendance, I told them about the young president's challenge that made such an impression on me when the cooperative was new.

I said, "President John F. Kennedy issued a call to organized labor to tackle 'the unfinished business of building and preserving affordable housing for working people." I said that all those years ago at Penn South, he told us, "This housing project demonstrates what labor can do for this city and this country." And today, half a century later, it still does. To be able to come back and give the residents a commitment to finance the renovation of their homes, well it felt to me like a way to memorialize President Kennedy and the spirit of the labor movement that built the cooperative.

Thanks to the unions that invest their pension dollars in the HIT, and in other union-friendly funds, we have the means to make strategic investments that fulfill our commitment to society and echo President Kennedy's long-ago call to action. We have the means for the union movement to make a positive impact on the shape of our communities and on the quality of life of the families who live there.

Projects like Penn South make me proud of my long association with the AFL-CIO Housing Investment Trust, and proud of my life in the labor movement that created it. With so many working people in this country still struggling to earn a living wage and to find decent, affordable places to live, the HIT's job-generating investments in affordable housing are as important today as they have ever been. The HIT helps the labor movement fulfill our commitment to union job creation and affordable housing – two of our most fundamental goals since the days of the AFL's first president, Samuel Gompers, a century ago.

Today's "Unfinished Business" As I See It. From my vantage point as HIT chairman emeritus, I know there is still much to be done – plenty of "unfinished business," as President Kennedy put it. Affordable housing is part of that. I intend to keep contributing to the HIT's efforts to harness the power of union capital to complete the work before us, to make life better for this and future generations.

The challenge ahead is to get more of labor's wealth at work building the economy and America's communities. If there were any doubts about where Wall Street's interests lie, they were settled in the Great Recession and its aftermath. Story after story came out about how so-called experts, who were in fact fiduciaries, robbed their clients or indulged in excesses of greed that would have shamed the oil barons of the nineteenth century. If nothing else came out of that economic collapse, it perhaps put an end to the fantasy that the best managers of America's $6 trillion of pension capital are the monied elites and their institutions. Organized Labor has to take a greater role in overseeing and managing its pension capital and all of America's pension assets.

As President of the AFL-CIO, I created the Capital Stewardship program to begin the oversight process. A successful program to this day, it ushered in a new era of shareholder activism. But the key word is "begin." There is so much more to do. It is work that is critical to whether this shift in wealth from working families to the elites can be tempered and reversed. If pension capital – the primary source of global capital – is managed without regard for the working people who create the pension capital and their communities, the income disparities so dramatic in American society today will only worsen. Such aggregation of the nation's wealth in so few hands eats at the heart of our democracy and jeopardizes our way of life. Having our pension capital managed with no accountability for the industries ruined or the local economies destroyed or the families financially wiped-out – that is the greatest threat to the long-term strength of our way of life.

What would I like to see set in motion that would reverse these trends? As I noted, the labor movement has to take charge of its capital through aggressive oversight and by example.

What we must do now is ensure that the safety nets that were put in place after the Great Depression remain in place or are restored. All working families should have retirement accounts. It should be a matter of law that employers must provide a funded pension program for their workforces. The most dire and immediate need is to get current pension plans fully funded in order to ensure that they are able to provide retirement income for workers. Chronic underfunding has been an unfortunate reality of pension plans for decades. In addition to having fully funded retirement plans, the beneficiaries should have a meaningful say in the management of their savings. Employers who move jobs out of the country should be required to fund all pension benefits for the affected employees who are vested in the company retirement plan. Employers, whether they are corporations or city governments, should not be able to reorganize away their pension obligations. Families should be able to pass on to their children their pension savings without penalties. In sum, we should have national policies to encourage the expansion of retirement income security for all working people and organized labor should fight to achieve this and prudently manage the capital as it is formed.

What the HIT and other labor sponsored vehicles do is excellent, but the labor community needs more vehicles like the HIT to invest in. There should be union-sponsored funds for venture capital investing, for creating new economies, for supporting start-up businesses, and for financing our infrastructure. Wherever capital is deployed, labor should be involved.

EPILOGUE

FOR KENNEDY

Right after my granddaughter was born in 2006, I ran into Ted Kennedy. He asked me her name, and I answered, "Kennedy." He looked at me, paused, and said very sternly: "Never let her forget the power of her name."

The next day he sent a gift: a diaper cover that said "Irish mist." That was the great thing about Teddy. One moment, he could be standing on the Senate floor, railing against special interests and the injustices of the world; the next, he could be laughing and caring for the people around him. He died in 2009, shortly before I left the AFL-CIO. Teddy was not only one of the labor movement's most consistent and influential supporters, but he was my long-time friend.[10]

Wisdom does not necessarily come with age, but what age does bring is an opportunity to reflect on one's life, the people that you have known and loved, the causes you care about, and the issues you fought for. My greatest concern for the future is the increasingly difficult economic struggle of America's working families. A strong and united American labor movement guards against a dramatic rise in income inequality and keeps intact the ladders that allow ordinary Americans to move up in the world. The fractures within the labor movement and the attacks from an increasingly well-funded and powerful opposition have threatened this great institution and the working people it represents.

The challenges to families are evident across the country and will continue to intensify if the unions empowered to speak and negotiate for working people continue to face loss of membership, unfair trade policies, and "Right to Work" laws. The Midwest is a case study in how closely linked the fates of the American labor movement and the working man and woman are. This region has seen a 43 percent loss in union membership since 1970 as good-paying jobs were lost to automation and flawed trade agreements. This has coincided with wage erosion as well as a dramatic rise in poverty rates in the region. When workers no longer have a seat at the bargaining table, inequality grows and the economy is weaker.

I think quite a bit now about the world my granddaughter Kennedy is inheriting. Despite our best efforts, we have left a lot of work unfinished. If I were a young person again, just arriving on the union scene, I would want to put the following things at the top of my agenda.

First of all, America still needs a raise. I know I have said this many times before. But the fact remains: America needed a raise in 1995 when I came on as AFL-CIO president, and America needs a raise now because economic insecurity has become an unhealthy fact of life. Unions play an outsized role in ensuring the prosperity of the middle class by building worker power, both at the workplace and in politics. Unfortunately, as union membership has declined as a portion of the workforce, so hasthe middle class' share of income.

The current Fight for 15 has brought the minimum wage fight to city halls and state houses across the country, and its energy and passion has captured the attention of the press and general public. The objective is laudable, and activists have won the phased-in adoption of a $15 minimum wage in California and New York, but we can't stop there. By allying with these workers and working to bring them into the labor movement, we can make bigger gains for all of the workers we represent.

John J. Sweeney

Next, we need trade and tax policies that support working people, not multinational corporations. We all live in a global economy, but trade policy should work for America's workers and raise standards for workers in all countries. President Trumka and the Democrats in Congress have released a blueprint on rewriting NAFTA to benefit working people. NAFTA has led to the loss of hundreds of thousands of good paying US jobs, many of which moved to Mexico, where workers are often denied their basic human rights and exposed to deplorable working conditions. The rewrite calls for, among other things, strengthening the workers' rights provisions and tightening the auto rule-of-origin requirements to ensure that more auto and auto-related jobs are incentivized to stay in the US.

The interest of the American worker, rather than the bottom line of corporations, should be at the center of any trade agreement moving forward. The only way to guarantee that happens is if labor has a seat at the table. This is also critical to the perception of our members who put their trust in us and contribute their hard earned money towards membership dues – they must see that we fight openly and effectively for good jobs.

We know that expanding the economic and political power of workers is essential to achieving a more just society. If we could mobilize all of our 12.5 million members to stand up for union values when their friends and neighbors parrot corporate criticism, to support elected officials who are working in their best interests, and to promote the union cause as a cause of working families – a public interest, not a special interest – we would solidify our base. We help millions of workers negotiate legally binding contracts that guarantee them good jobs with decent pay and benefits. Those union contracts keep standards up for everybody. And we use our political muscle to support officials and policies that promise to create an economy that works for all working people. That is the message the public has to hear.

Solidarity within the labor movement is critical in the new political landscape of super PACs and corporate union busting. Solidarity – the idea that common interests and mutual obligations unite working people – is the key to our future success. Rich Trumka is making progress. Since 2009, UNITE HERE, the Laborers, and the UFCW have re-affiliated with the AFL-CIO. But as a labor historian once put it, it is easier to sing about solidarity than to achieve it. We cannot ignore the fact that unions still represent 10.7 percent of the workforce – and even that is under constant attack. We must work together to effect change and unite behind our shared values.

Finally, we must continue to use our pension capital to make investments that advance our goals. That means actively participating in the investment decisions of our pension and benefit plans, supporting investments that promote union jobs and strengthen our communities, and participating in corporate governance to make companies more accountable to working families and their communities.

I have talked about what priorities I would pursue if I were coming up as a young labor leader today. But I have come to realize that I am truly a person of my time. I was born to a family with little material wealth, but I was fortunate to have been raised with the values of family, faith, and union so deeply embedded in me – to have learned at an early age the significance of community and collective action in achieving social justice – and to have been inspired and directed to my life's calling by an understanding of the sanctity of each individual, no matter how humble. Whatever success I have achieved in my career has been built on that foundation. But today we live in a world so full of egocentric leaders, poll-driven principles, and materialistic pursuits. I wonder if I were a young person coming of age today, would I still have been able to find the moral understanding and spiritual drive to serve the needs of working people as I was so fortunate to do with my life? Would this "bookish cleric," as the New York Times described me back in the day, have had the same opportunities to rise step by step to the top, to earn such respect, to lead a national movement? I certainly hope so. And I believe the labor movement continues to be one of the best places to find a spiritually enriching career.

Much work lies ahead for the committed young labor leaders who are striving to build a better world for the working families of tomorrow. But what I think they will want to do, and must do, is face the economic challenges of the time head-on. They must use those challenges as opportunities. When you have a good strategy, good community support, workers in motion, and a story defined around values, you can transform those opportunities into victories and reshape the future for America's working families.

That will not be easy. But it is so important. My granddaughter Kennedy and the members of her generation – and generations yet to come – are counting on you.

*In 1979, I was honored to be chosen to lead the NYC
Labor Day Parade as Grand Marshal.*

*As President of 32BJ, I attended the Executive Council Meeting of the
AFL-CIO with my family in 1977, the year 32B and 32J merged.*

*Protesting apartheid at the South African embassy in Washington,
D.C. in 1985. I later allowed myself to be arrested along with other
demonstrators to publicize South Africa's repressive policies.*

*Shaking hands with South Africa's Archbishop Desmond
Tutu outside his country's embassy in Washington.*

*Chatting with Coretta Scott King at an 1199-
SEIU healthcare conference in 1981.*

*Watching the Reverend Jesse Jackson as he tries out a floor buffer, a device often used by our members. This took place
during a 1987 SEIU executive board meeting in Washington
where we discussed Jackson's 1988 run for president.*

John J. Sweeney

Meeting with President Clinton in the Oval Office. He was an accessible president, and we had many conversations on policy issues.

Introducing the new first lady, Hillary Clinton, to SEIU Vice President and rights activist Ophelia McFadden at our 1993 Lobby Day in Washington, D.C.

*Talking with Nelson Mandela in 1991, a year after
he was freed from prison in South Africa.*

ACKNOWLEDGEMENTS

I am grateful to those who have stood with me in the fight for the rights and integrity of working people - a group that includes presidents and police, janitors and journey workers. Without these individuals, the Labor Movement would not exist and I would have no story to tell. To all my dedicated staff, I thank you for your loyalty, hardwork, and friendship. I could not have done it without you. I am grateful to Rich Trumka who has led the North American Labor Movement with great strength since 2009 and the many labor leaders across the country who have fought an increasingly difficult battle to organize and advocate for working men and women. Your commitment inspires; your work is invaluable.

This book began with a series of taped interviews in 2010 and has evolved and pushed forward with the help of many dedicated and talented individuals. Denise Mitchell and Bob Welsh, among my closest advisers during my career, served as editors and sounding boards throughout the book writing process. They pushed the project forward and were involved every step of the way. Grace Palladino, a researcher and historian with great knowledge of the labor movement, and Ann Kay, a gifted writer and long-time member of the labor movement, both also helped bring my story alive. The AFL-CIO Housing Investment Trust made the book logistically possible, and for that I am grateful to its leader and my friend, Steve Coyle. I would also like to thank Katie Rosenthal, who was a wonderful coordinator for this book. Kate Donlan, who designed the cover, and Erica Hunter, who assisted in editing, also helped to make the book a reality.

Above all, I must thank my wife Maureen for her love and support in this endeavor and throughout our marriage. Our children, John and Trish, and granddaughter, Kennedy, are a tremendous source of joy and pride and have inspired me in all that I have done.

ENDNOTES:
FURTHER REFLECTIONS

¹Keeping a Handle on Local 32BJ

After I moved to Washington, D.C., and became president of SEIU, I liked to do whatever I could for 32BJ, especially when the union faced tough negotiations. For example, at about the time of some important building services negotiations in New York City in the early '90s, I was invited up to West Point to speak to the Ways and Means Committee of the House of Representatives. This was when Dan Rostenkowski was the chair. They were having a retreat. Since Rostenkowski's issue was health care, I went up to West Point on a Saturday because I thought that this was a great opportunity for me to speak to this group of leadership from the Congress on this important issue.

I was there for the opening, but I wasn't scheduled to speak till the next morning. So Saturday evening I had somebody take me back to New York City so that I could participate with the 32BJ committee on their negotiations. The negotiations involved around 30,000 workers in the apartment buildings and 30,000 in the office buildings.

I got to New York City around ten o'clock at night. I sat with the committee and they reviewed what the last offer was. I put my own two words into the discussion. I wanted to go over issues like what had to be done for the sake of moving negotiations, what had to be bargained, or what had to be changed, if change was necessary. Being there to have my input into those discussions I felt was important. At the point when 32BJ's president – Gus Bevona, at the time – and the Real Estate Board head were ready to go at it, one on one, I said, "I'm going to lay down for a while. Wake me up whenever you need something."

I wasn't woken up until about three o'clock in the morning. I was just lying on top of the bed with my clothes on and everything, so I was ready. Gus wanted me to come spend a little time on this, so I did. Around six o'clock, I guess, I figured that they weren't going to make much progress, so I said, "I'm going to go back to West Point and do my talk, and I'll be available this afternoon."

The same guy had the car waiting outside and took me back to West Point to the Thayer Hotel. When I got there, some of the congressmen were down having their breakfast. I went down and I sat at the table that Charlie Rangel was sitting at, and he said, "How are negotiations going with 32BJ?" His congressional district was one of the large districts in the city of New York. So I told him that I thought the negotiations were going very well, and that it would be pretty safe to say that either there would be a settlement Sunday night or there would be a strike.

I said, "I was there for most of the night."

"You were there?"

I said, "Yeah. I had somebody pick me up after your dinner discussions yesterday. I got to the negotiations just in time to do some meetings and to see how I could be helpful. Six a.m., I was back in the car and the same person drove me back here so that I could have breakfast with you."

He said to me, "I can't make up my mind whether you're just so dedicated that you would do that or you're crazy."

²My Introduction to the AFL-CIO's International Program

Ever since the end of World War II, the AFL and then the AFL-CIO had promoted a policy of free trade unionism that was based on an agenda of anti-communism abroad and full employment at home. At the time, it was not that unusual to oppose the Soviet Union or to expect government support for our international efforts, either in our fight to restore democratic trade union centers in Germany, France, or Italy, for example, or in our call for defense spending that many believed would help us at home as well as abroad.

No one was more dedicated to free trade unions – and more opposed to communist rule – than the AFL-CIO's first president, George Meany, who had watched the inter-union fights with communist factions that tore apart unions like the ILGWU in the 1920s and '30s. So it was not surprising that in 1949 he helped organize the International Confederation of Free Trade Unions, or ICFTU, as an anti-communist, pro-full employment coalition. It was also not surprising that when he felt that communist labor leaders had too much influence in the ICFTU, he took the AFL-CIO out in 1969. When he had the same dissatisfaction with the International Labour Organization, or ILO, a few years later, he helped get the U.S. to withdraw.

Lane Kirkland, George's successor at the AFL-CIO, was just as interested in the international scene but he took a different approach as president. For instance, he had been going to ILO annual conferences since the late 1950s, and he never really agreed with George's decision to withdraw. Where George would say, "We don't accept the price of coexistence with gangsters," Lane believed that "All sinners belong in the church." His approach was more diplomatic and in a sense more pragmatic, because if the AFL-CIO wanted to have any influence, it could not remain outside. And that being the case, it was not too long after Lane succeeded George as AFL-CIO president in 1979 that we were back in both organizations. While I was serving as president of SEIU, Lane gave me the opportunity to get directly involved in international programs as a delegate to the ILO.

Maureen and I had the opportunity to meet with Lech Walesa, leader of the Polish free trade union movement, Solidarność, in Gdansk, Poland, 1989.

Irving Brown was Lane's director of international affairs while I was developing my interests in this area, and he was a controversial figure to say the least. But I learned a lot from him and his experiences. Some people called him the godfather of the AFL-CIO's overseas operations. He had been the labor movement's emissary to Europe after World War II, and he played a highly recognized role in rallying support among unions there for the Marshall Plan to promote recovery in Western Europe, as well as in establishing the ICFTU. He was very active and respected by the labor movement in countries that were our allies. I know that there are some who strongly criticized Brown and presumed he was involved with the CIA, but I never saw any real proof one way or the other. He was a very smart man – someone that Lane, in particular, relied on and trusted. And it was interesting that conservatives like Utah's senator, Orrin Hatch – with whom we shared very few points of agreement – had a high respect for Brown because of his battles with communists and supported, in those days, the AFL-CIO's international affairs program.

By the time I became president of the AFL-CIO, I felt that our foreign affairs policies needed a new direction. The Solidarity Center that I established to replace the older foreign policy institutes served to broaden the AFL-CIO's focus from containing communism to promoting the rights of workers to organize and developing greater coordination with others around the globe in advocating for workers' rights.

[3]Lane Kirkland and Solidarity

When Lane Kirkland became president of the AFL-CIO in 1979, I do not think anyone was surprised that his style was different from that of his predecessor, George Meany. His personality was different, his prior experience was different. Lane Kirkland was a college graduate and had served in the U.S. Merchant Marine as a member of the Organization of Masters, Mates, and Pilots. He was more of an intellectual than George appeared to be, although George was a very wise, self-educated man. Lane did not take long to establish himself as a world labor leader. He brought a welcome knowledge in his own right and some great talents that had been very helpful to George when Lane served as his assistant and then as AFL-CIO secretary-treasurer.

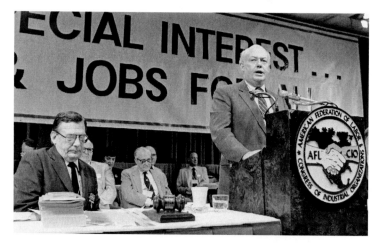

*Addressing an AFL-CIO gathering, with AFL-CIO
President Lane Kirkland (seated at left).*

Lane had a strong interest in international affairs, particularly with the growing influence of communism in Europe and its impact on free trade unionism and human rights. When the Polish trade union Solidarity, or Solidarność, challenged the communist government and was forced underground in the early '80s, Lane organized a fund and raised millions of dollars to assist them. He really helped keep them alive until they were allowed to resurface in Poland almost 10 years later.

[4]A "Rare Bird" at the Davos Economic Forum

I became the first AFL-CIO president to participate in the World Economic Forum, which met annually in Davos, Switzerland. Union leaders were seen there so infrequently, in fact, that when I attended the meeting in 1998, the *New York Times* headline read, "Rare Bird in Davos." The story went on to describe me as a "water buffalo in a herd of elephants." Klaus Schwab, who founded and runs the organization, was somebody that I had met through my international work, so when I was invited for the first time in 1997 I was delighted to accept, because I knew that very few union leaders attended Davos meetings. Schwab really wanted more labor participation, so we did not have to pay the registration fee that corporations and others had to pay.

The goal of these meetings was to get world leaders talking together about how to improve the state of the world. I saw Davos as an opportunity to meet some of our own corporate leaders, but also some of our own government representatives. There are probably about 15 or 20 members of Congress who attend, members of the cabinet, as well as the president of the United States. Bill Clinton went a couple of times when I was there. But it was quite a different experience for me to walk the halls and say hello to people like the CEO of Caterpillar, Inc., while we were still embroiled in a pretty serious battle. At Davos I could chat with chief executives and world leaders in a way that I could never do at home.

The speech I gave in 1998, on a panel with philanthropist George Soros and Brazil's president Fernando Cardoso, was a good example of labor's global agenda. We were talking about the collapse of the Asian economy and its impact on the rest of the world. They both thought that strong economic growth would solve all problems. But I argued that growth without social justice was a disaster in the making. We needed a new era of reform that would seek greater accountability from capital and empowerment for workers and citizens. No one was looking to stop globalization in its tracks. We just wanted coordinated efforts to stimulate growth, regulate currency and capital speculation, and extend labor and democratic rights as part of the response to the Asian collapse. And we wanted people to realize that if the International Monetary Fund bailed out the speculators and banks that caused the problem in the first place, while enforcing austerity measures on everyone else, it would just reinforce the behavior it was trying to cure. People talked about the moral hazard of rewarding speculators and banks, I said. But very few mentioned the "immoral hazard" of forcing working people across the world to pay the price – in layoffs, declining wages, and increasing insecurity.

Newt Gingrich was also in Davos, and at one of the sessions, he said my thinking was out-of-date, that I was a throwback to sit-down strikers of the 1930s. But he never understood what I was talking about. The AFL-CIO was not opposed to trade agreements, just those trade agreements that left workers out. Take NAFTA. One CEO told me that as productivity went up in Mexico, wages would rise. And I told him that, in my experience, the jobs NAFTA created in Mexico and the U.S. were low wage jobs, and in Mexico, the lowest of the low.

When people would ask me why I was so interested in going to Davos, I usually told them the story about the first year I was there, when Jack Welch, the CEO of General Electric, invited me to have breakfast. I was happy to do that. I had been doing some labor-management discussions with him in Washington, D.C. I was surprised, though, when he told me he did not enjoy coming to Davos. When I asked why he came, he said, "Where else can I set up the meetings with my peers, with governments, with whomever in four or five days? It would take me months to set up that." And it was so true.

So, the exchanges were very rewarding: meeting with Jack, with George Soros, with Bill Gates. It was a pleasure to have Bono, the Irish rock star and activist, come over and chat about poverty in the developing world. Davos certainly gave me a chance to share an opinion that most of the participants probably did not hear very often.

[5]Thoughts About My Relationship with Andy Stern

I was angry and deeply disappointed when Andy Stern and his Change to Win coalition tore apart the house of labor. Ever since Andy led the Service Employees International Union – my union – out of the AFL-CIO in 2005, people have asked if I ever regretted giving him his start when I was president of SEIU. And the answer is an unqualified "No."

I had high expectations of Andy because I knew how talented he would be, and he delivered on a lot of that. He was a good leader in Pennsylvania when he represented the social workers. He was a good organizing director for SEIU. Back then, Andy did not really express much of the visionary ideas that he came to later, and I am not sure that he had developed the ideas and the proposals that he articulated as he grew in the organization.

[6]Pension Reforms

In my many years in the labor movement I have learned that retirement benefits are one of the most import benefits that union membership provides. Security in retirement through Social Security and pension funds has kept millions of retirees and elderly out of poverty in the last century. Union pension funds have been a huge part of the retirement wealth landscape in the last hundred years. But today many union pension funds are threatened due in part to recessions and to a smaller ratio between workers contributing to the plans and retirees drawing benefits – not due to mismanagement as many politicians would have you believe. In the last thirty-five years, pension assets have only ever been fully funded for one year, in 2000 right before the dot-com bubble burst.

One of the most critical problems facing the continued solvency of union pension funds is a lack of capital in the Pension Benefit Guaranty Corporation, a kind of insurance for pension funds, to cover benefits should multiple pension funds fail. The Multiemployer Pension Reform Act of 2014 focused on helping critically underfunded pension plans to restructure or merge to avoid resorting to drastic cuts in benefits to stay afloat. While it did increase the amount of money that must be contributed to the PBGC and allowed the PBGC to help pension funds merge it also unfortunately allows funds to cut benefits, placing the burden on retirees and the PBGC is still at risk of collapse in ten years. There is more work to be done.

While these recent reforms will help pension plans in the short term, they are only a band-aid. The only thing that will help in the long term is to make sure that every working American has a retirement plan and that those plans are managed by prudent investors who embody the goals and values of the American labor movement. We have to make sure that we invest our retirement funds responsibly in ourselves and our communities. It is hard work to make socially responsible investments but it is a strategy that every fund manager should aspire to.

[7]George Meany and the Civil Rights Movement

I like to remember that "We Shall Overcome," the great ballad of the civil rights movement, was first used as a protest song by union members – striking tobacco workers – as they marched on their picket line in Charleston, South Carolina in 1945. By the 1950s the song was adopted as the anthem of the civil rights movement, sung at marches and sit-ins in the struggle for justice and racial equality. George Meany helped make the AFL-CIO part of that struggle.

George Meany was a strong, early, and unapologetic supporter of the civil rights movement. He helped project Dr. Martin Luther King, Jr., onto the national stage through the AFL-CIO's financial and legal support for the Southern Christian Leadership Conference, led by Dr. King. In 1960, at the invitation of President Meany, Dr. King addressed the AFL-CIO convention. This invitation gave Dr. King an important platform for advancing the civil rights movement at a time when many were still shying from his cause and some others were out to vilify him.

President Meany put the AFL-CIO's weight behind the ground-breaking civil rights legislation that Congress was considering in the early 1960s, insisting that the Civil Rights Act of 1964 include provisions for ending workplace discrimination. Those provisions became the basis for Title VII of the civil rights law.

There is a poignant photo in the AFL-CIO's offices, taken at President Johnson's signing of the Civil Rights Act of 1964, which shows President Meany and Dr. King seated together among the dignitaries. Frankly I do not think George Meany has gotten enough credit for what he did for the civil rights movement.

[8]Small Investments with a Big Impact

Two of the most memorable investments the HIT made under the Community Investment Corporation Demonstration Program were for HIV/AIDS victims and very low income families. The demonstration program allowed HUD to provide capital assistance to projects serving low income residents. In the mid-1990s, the HIT financed the rehabilitation of 64 single family housing properties in seven New Jersey cities. The HIT proposed a new financing structure that HUD adopted, so these scattered single-family projects could all be financed as one "multifamily" mortgage loan. That innovative loan structure made the project financially feasible. The HIT invested $1.8 million in the project and also directed another $8.4 million to the project through HUD's Section 8 assistance. The rehabilitated properties had an urgent mission: to provide safe and affordable housing for families that had members living with HIV/AIDS. At the time, misinformation about the disease caused rampant housing discrimination against people affected by HIV/AIDS, a grave injustice, so these housing units coupled with social services were desperately needed.

The second project was El Azteca, an award-winning affordable housing project that the HIT financed in Laredo, Texas. That city, located on the Texas-Mexico border, had a poverty rate of more than 35 percent at the time El Azteca was built in 1996. El Azteca's 50 housing units offered new accommodations for some of Laredo's poorest residents, many of whom had been living in ramshackle settlements outside of town without running water or neighborhood infrastructure.

[9]Remembering 9/11 as AFL-CIO President

I remember driving in to work on September 11, 2001, a beautiful fall morning. I was coming down Massachusetts Avenue in D.C. around a quarter to nine or so when the news came on the radio that a plane had gone into the World Trade Center. Like so many others, I thought that it was a small plane and never realized that it could be as devastating as it was. Then a plane hit the second tower, and I learned that the Pentagon had been hit and that a plane heading towards Washington had gone down in Pennsylvania. So this beautiful fall morning turned out to be one of the most serious days in my life, in all our lives, really. The loss of life – including many union lives – was staggering.

The saddest part, for me, was to go down into that hole, a couple of days later, and to have the chance to meet with people who were involved in the rescue, who were dealing with the losses, helping with the families, and so on. I had the chance to observe the bravery and dedication of so many different crafts and different groups of workers, the Firefighters, the Iron Workers, the Operating Engineers, the Laborers, the EMTs, and so many others. Across the street from Ground Zero, there was a building that had not been damaged too much, which was where the cots were for these workers to get an hour's rest during the 24-hour shifts that they were performing. We will live with that horrible memory throughout our lives, and we will never forget the role that workers played after such devastation, those who sacrificed their lives or who were permanently disabled, those who worked so hard to try to save their brothers and sisters. There are so many stories that can be told, but none can truly tell how courageous and heroic these people were and how much our country owes to them.

One of the men who was escorting us around when we went down there was a Firefighter officer. In the middle of our conversation, one of his peers came over and whispered something in his ear. It was about one of the Firefighters in his battalion; his body had been found. And to see this fellow break down and then go off to where they had found his friend, it was so sad. I was told that he had been escorting the body of every single Firefighter that had come out.

My own union, 32BJ, lost more than 100 members. These were folks who were service workers, janitors, security guards, people who worked in the restaurants at the top of the World Trade Center. The Firefighters lost almost 400 men and women, the worst tragedy in their history, the Police lost nearly 100. The Communications Workers lost 181 members. The International Brotherhood of Electrical Workers, the Carpenters,

AFSCME, they all lost workers on the job. Three union Teachers were on the plane that left from Dulles Airport, and the Flight Attendants and Pilots had 35 members on all four planes that were turned into lethal weapons by the hijackers. They were all our brothers and sisters, mothers, fathers, children, friends and neighbors – working people who had started the day with the same hopes and expectations that we all had that morning.

And later, it was shocking that we had to fight to get extended medical benefits paid for those workers at Ground Zero. We worked with the New York congressional delegation for years for legislation to help not only these Firefighters, but the hundreds of thousands of others who were exposed to dust from the collapsed World Trade Center. At the time they were led to believe that the air was safe, but a monitoring program based at Mount Sinai Medical Center found that about four in ten of its patients from the site had breathing problems, including asthma, and many suffered mental health problems. Six years after the attacks, many of them still had not gotten the medical and financial help they needed. A congresswoman from New York City, Carolyn Maloney, had introduced a health and compensation bill that we strongly supported and which I myself held a number of meetings on, but it took months and months and months. Sadly, nothing happened until we had a friendlier administration in Washington. So it was a tough, tough time, and it still is.

[10]Remembering My Friend Ted Kennedy

Ted Kennedy and I had a good friendship and a high regard for each other – about as high as any two as friends could have. Ted understood labor issues, not just in theory but he had a deep and abiding empathy for the needs of ordinary people. As a senator, he mastered whatever it was he was working on; he understood all the key parts of a bill and what it took to get it approved. There was simply no one like him in the Senate.

Meeting with Senator Ted Kennedy when I testified at Senate hearings on the 1987 health care bill, Washington, D.C.

One of the last times we met was in January 2009. I had called him to see if we could get together, as we usually did after the holidays. I knew he was very ill, so I said I would come and meet him at his office or his home, wherever was best for him. He said, "No, I want to come to the AFL-CIO," and he did, bringing his two dogs with him. He sat with me and Bill Samuel, our legislative director; Larry Cohen, president of the Communications Workers; and Senator Tom Harkin and Congressman George Miller, who would introduce the Employee Free Choice Act in March. For two hours we talked about health care and labor legislation reform, planning strategy for the fight ahead.

In March 2015, Maureen and I had the privilege of being invited by President Obama's Secretary of Labor, Tom Perez, to a special dedication in memory of Ted Kennedy at the U.S. Department of Labor in Washington, D.C. Secretary Perez had served on Senator Kennedy's staff on the Senate Labor Committee. He told us of an episode when Senator Strom Thurmond, the arch-conservative Republican from South Carolina, had prevailed on a vote against Ted. After the vote, Senator Thurmond said: "Ted, I hate everything you stand for. But you are still my friend!" It was that way with many others from across the political aisle, among them Orrin Hatch and John McCain. Ted lobbied hard for his legislative priorities, but it was never personal. I miss that powerful voice in the Senate.

Although he came from wealth and privilege, he was one of us, a man of the people, all the people.

INDEX

Symbols

Index

UNITE HERE 15, 135, 136, 142, 143, 157, 161, 179
Unite to Win 130
University of Ulster, Northern Ireland 166

V

Valdes, Chuck 55
Van Arsdale, Harry, Jr. 34, 35
Vancouver Labor Council 109
Vietnam War 173
Voice@Work 113, 116

W

Wagner, Robert 21
Wall Street Journal 119, 155
Ward, Cecil 24, 38, 43
Washington Post 64, 65, 82, 88
Waters, Maxine 48
Weinlein, Tony 41, 42
Welch, Jack 206
Wellstone, Paul 76
Welsh, Robert 47, 162
Westchester County Democratic Committee 18
Westchester Glen Island Casino 20
White, Robert 163
Wilhelm, John 135, 138
Winning for Working Families 137
Working America 127, 128, 129, 143, 144, 161
Working Families Vote 2008 145
Workmen's Circle Multi-Care Center 180
Works Progress Administration 2
World Bank 64, 91
World Economic Forum 207
World Trade Organization 112
World War II 203
Wynn, William 60

X

Xavier Labor Relations Institute, New

York City, New York 12, 17, 166

Y

Yokich, Stephen P. 110
Young, Thomas 24, 30, 56

IMAGE CREDITS

Page 5 AFL-CIO

Page 10 Family photograph

Page 19 Family photograph

Page 36 Walter P. Reuther Library, Archives of Labor and Urban Affairs, Wayne State University, Credit: Ben-Ness Cameras and Photo Studio

Page 40 Walter P. Reuther Library, Archives of Labor and Urban Affairs, Wayne State University

Page 43 Walter P. Reuther Library, Archives of Labor and Urban Affairs, Wayne State University

Page 54 Walter P. Reuther Library, Archives of Labor and Urban Affairs, Wayne State University

Page 73 Walter P. Reuther Library, Archives of Labor and Urban Affairs, Wayne State University

Page 89 AFL-CIO

Page 99 Walter P. Reuther Library, Archives of Labor and Urban Affairs, Wayne State University

Page 102 AFL-CIO

Page 149 AFL-CIO

Page 160 AFL-CIO

Page 162 Family photograph

Page 167 Family photograph

Page 170 AFL-CIO

Page 194 Family photograph

Page 194 Family photograph

Page 195 Walter P. Reuther Library, Archives of Labor and Urban Affairs, Wayne State University, Credit: Ray Crowell/Page One Photo

Page 195 Walter P. Reuther Library, Archives of Labor and Urban Affairs, Wayne State University

Page 196 Walter P. Reuther Library, Archives of Labor and Urban Affairs, Wayne State University

Page 196 Walter P. Reuther Library, Archives of Labor and Urban Affairs, Wayne State University

Page 197 AFL-CIO

Page 197 Walter P. Reuther Library, Archives of Labor and Urban Affairs, Wayne State University, Credit: Bill Burke/Page One Photo

Page 198 AFL-CIO

Page 203 AFL-CIO

Page 204 AFL-CIO

Page 213 Walter P. Reuther Library, Archives of Labor and Urban Affairs, Wayne State University